The Fragrance of a Godly Woman

The Fragrance of a Godly Woman

Practical Ways to Become a
Woman of Influence

FATIMA SIBANDA

Sibanda Publishing

Dedication

To my husband, Osien.
Without your support this book would have remained a dream. Thank you.

To my two lovely daughters,
Ayanda Blessing and Realeboga Phumzile.
May you grow up to be godly women who will spread a godly fragrance to the nations.

A catalogue record for this book is available from the British Library.

Published in the United Kingdom by Sibanda Publishing
ISBN: 978-0-9561175-0-2

Endorsements

The value of *The Fragrance of a Godly Woman* is embedded in the practical insight it sheds. Fatima is not hesitant to expose her personal shortcomings. However, she is also incisive about how she could have improved her lot. She tackles issues about women and their self-esteem and self-worth. Personal influence is thoroughly dealt with. All of us have got it, in different measures.

In my experience of working with women for years, apart from their health issues, women tend to bear the brunt of circumstances which are beyond their control, whether it be from broken relationships, failure to conceive, miscarriages or the stigma in certain cultures of giving birth only to girls. They shoulder all these responsibilities, sometimes not properly equipped, and consequently they drown in the emotional turmoil that comes with them. *Fragrance* sheds great light on many of these emotional issues, some of which should not actually be issues at all.

Dr Emmanuel C Majachani MBCHB, FCOG (SA)
Resident Obstetrician and Gynaecologist at Sunninghill Hospital
Chairman of Husbands Agape Fellowship International
Johannesburg, South Africa

The Fragrance of a Godly Woman is a very powerful tool, which can liberate women from all walks of life. It helped me realise that the value of a woman is not in her bank balance, not in the circumstances in which she finds herself, nor in what people think or say about her. The value of a woman comes from the One who created her. *Fragrance* is a must-read; it will enable you to face life's challenges and bring out your godly aroma as a blessing to those in your sphere of influence. This book will add value to any woman's library.

Edith Majachani
Chairperson of Gracious Women Fellowship International
Johannesburg, South Africa

The Fragrance of a Godly Woman is broad in its subject matter and there is something in it for everyone. If you're married, you will learn how to improve your marriage. If you're a mother, you will learn how to become a better steward of the children God has given you. If you're single, you'll learn how to serve God wholeheartedly as you focus on Him. If you're broken, it will help you receive healing and move on with your life. And if you're a man, it will give you insight into how women are designed and bring you understanding of their function in life. More importantly, as a child of God, you will learn how to practically love God and love others as you love yourself. That's what's great about this book – it's practical – and you may identify with many of the real-life stories.

Fragrance is an amazing book. I am passionate about its principles because as I've watched Fatima, my mentor, apply them in her life, I've seen that they are working. I have also been applying them in my life and they've helped me to deal with issues from my past and embrace my future. I've learnt to confidently celebrate who God has created me to be.

Loulita Di Somma

Protégé
Bristol, United Kingdom

Contents

A charge to keep I have

A charge to keep I have, a God to glorify,
A never-dying soul to save, and fit it for the sky.

To serve the present age, my calling to fulfil;
O may it all my powers engage to do my Master's will!

Arm me with jealous care, as in Thy sight to live,
And oh, Thy servant, Lord, prepare a strict account to give!

Help me to watch and pray, and on Thyself rely,
Assured, if I my trust betray, I shall forever die.

(Charles Wesley, 1707–1788)

In loving memory of my late mum, Bessie Chimkupete, affectionately known as Gogo – the first woman whose godly fragrance influenced my life.
She was a hard-working woman who loved her family passionately and served her generation humbly.
I thank God for giving me such a mum.
Before she went home to be with the Lord she gave me this hymn as a reminder of the call of God on my life.

Foreword

In my ministry of over two decades, I have often had to help women who have found themselves in challenging situations which could have been avoided. My wife and I have been deeply moved as we have ministered to hurting women of different nations, backgrounds and walks of life, whose problems are similar across the board. I believe that the book you are holding, *The Fragrance of a Godly Woman*, will help many.

The pressures of today's society have led to some women accepting degradation, abuse, exploitation, violence, to name but a few, as their lot in life. Many of them are going through things that have arisen through no fault of theirs, yet they feel as if they are cursed with no remedy. There are many men today whose actions reveal that they do not appreciate the wives God has given them. If you have a wife, you need to see her as the embodiment of God's favour in your life. *Proverbs 18:22* says, *'He who finds a wife finds a good thing, and obtains favor from the Lord.'* Some have daughters who are God's grace and goodness personified, but because they are the 'wrong' gender, they are neither accepted nor valued.

Many women have undermined the treasure which God has invested in them, the treasure that was placed there to benefit humanity. It is difficult for some to see themselves the way God sees them. In *The Fragrance of a Godly Woman*, the author takes us back to Genesis to discover God's original purpose for women in a clear and informative manner. It liberates women and shows them how to use their uniqueness to have a positive influence in their world.

Today, the Holy Spirit is raising up women of stature who will help restore the battered image of women back to the original image created by God. I believe that Fatima Sibanda is one of those voices that God is using to bring dignity to women of this generation. I have witnessed first-hand the deep compassion that the author has for women who are hurting as well as for dysfunctional marriages. She writes out of a wellspring of love for God's people.

Fatima succinctly brings a fresh and clear perspective to the way in which women ought to view themselves as well as the way in which the world ought to view them. She teaches that, in the same way that perfume is made up of different ingredients, some of which are bitter, so is the life of a fragrant woman. When all the bitter experiences are placed into God's hands, she becomes a beautiful perfume. She exudes the fragrance of God to the world around her.

This book is not just for women. It will also help men to understand and value women. Do you have a wife? Do you have a daughter? Do you have a sister? Do you have female friends or colleagues? If you want to know how God expects you to treat women; if you want to learn to appreciate women; then this book is a must-read.

Eric Bapetel

Senior Pastor, Every Nation Church
Midrand, Johannesburg, South Africa
Author of *Jewels of Truth for Achievers*

A word from the author

The word 'woman' often triggers mixed responses from people in various walks of life. Some consider a woman to be a weak thing, whilst others blame her for the fall of mankind. In some quarters, the word 'woman' is a derogatory term used to insult a man who is considered weak or a coward, a failure, a man who doesn't know how to carry out his responsibilities. Others think of a woman as a sex object. The good thing is that these sentiments are not universally accepted and they are not God's Word. A woman is God's special gift to mankind, created for a specific purpose and designed to fulfil different roles in life.

As a minister of the Gospel, I have travelled to many places and have met women from different ethnic, racial and religious backgrounds. What I have observed is that they all face similar challenges, only packaged in different ways. I have also noticed that the effects of the problems experienced by many women are essentially the same. For example, a woman who has been raped is confronted with the same emotional pain as any other woman who has been raped, regardless of her background, race, education or social standing. Divorce and rejection have a similar effect on women, no matter which part of the world they live in. Pain cannot be classified according to one's status or social background. Pain is pain, and it always hurts.

Despite the numerous challenges facing women globally, within each woman is hidden a beautiful and unique fragrance which is waiting to be released in order to bless others. When this extraordinary potential is tapped into, given the right environment, and is properly developed, it can impact and change this world for good right across generations. Take for example Mother Teresa, who dedicated her life to the cause of the poor, the sick, the orphaned and the dying. She was not born a world-changer but became one because her potential was tapped into and properly developed. Even now her fragrance still lingers and people continue to benefit from the work that she did during her lifetime.

For many, many years this book has been brewing in my heart. My prayer is that it empowers today's woman to discover her true value, to be encouraged to release her godly fragrance and to make a difference in this world. I thank the Lord for the grace to finally write this book.

Woman, it's time to arise from your disappointments, heartaches and frustrations. It's time to rise up from situations that have tried to place limitations on you and redefine you into something that God never originally meant you to be. You are designed for greatness. You can achieve great things that will bless your generation and generations to come. God bless you richly as you choose to release your godly fragrance.

Fatima Sibanda

CHAPTER ONE

God's original fragrance in you

When my dad and mum, Fredrick and Bessie Chimkupete, got married, the community in which they lived placed a much higher value on sons than daughters. Sons were considered to be precious since they would be the heirs who would carry on the family name and continue to support the family in the future.

Sons were also valuable because they would help run the household, look after the cattle and crops, fight the enemy, hunt, provide for the family, as well as protect the girls. It was deemed very necessary, not only to have sons, but also to educate them, since educating them meant a long-term investment for yourself.

My parents, being Christians, didn't hold to these beliefs that sons were of greater value than daughters. They believed that every child is a special gift from God and should therefore be loved, cherished and invested in, regardless of gender. Living in an environment that strongly promoted having sons rather than daughters proved challenging for them, especially when their firstborn was a girl! Although they celebrated the birth of their daughter, Prisca, the rest of the community wasn't impressed. In their eyes, my parents had failed to produce an heir.

When it was time for Prisca to start school, some of my dad's friends discouraged and isolated him because he was doing something which was considered a taboo – to educate a female. It was generally accepted at that time that instead of giving a woman a formal education, she should rather concentrate on domestic chores as training for her future. People believed that a woman's destiny was marriage and educating her would simply be a waste of money. When she got married, she would leave her family to join another one, so there was no point of investing in her for someone else's benefit.

Although my dad was aware of all the negative voices offering their opinions concerning Prisca's education, he and my mum made the decision to follow their conviction. My dad made an arrangement with his employer to be paid in advance so that he could send Prisca to school and pay her school fees on time.

Once again, much to the disappointment of the extreme chauvinists in their community, my parents' second and thirdborn were also girls – Lilian and Florence (sadly Florence passed away when she was still very young). With the arrival of their fourth child, however, there was great excitement! Peter was born and the community celebrated the fact that my parents finally had an heir. But the excitement soon fizzled out because after Peter came Constance, Tracy, Sevy, me (Fatima) and finally Joyce – in total eight girls and one boy.

Can you imagine if my parents succumbed to the male chauvinistic ideas and prejudice held against girls? It would have meant that only one out of their eight children would be considered worthy of an education. If they had discriminated against their daughters because of their gender, Peter would be the only one with an education today. I'm grateful for the stance that my parents took to invest in all of us, as costly as it was. While my dad's colleagues would have fun with their salaries, he sacrificed all his earnings for the education of all his children. My mum did not sit on her hands and wait for her husband to carry this load alone, but used her industrious hands to come up with income-generating ventures to assist my dad. Today we are all educated and excelling in our different disciplines and fields, impacting the lives of people around us.

Although my story goes back a number of years, the reality is that some of the social values and traditions within my parents' community still exist in many places today. There are women in the world who are treated as second-class citizens and have no voice. They are often seen as weak and unable to function without a man to depend on. Some women don't even get to choose who they will marry. The choice is made for them. Often they are only informed after the arrangements have been made, and they are expected to enter into and enjoy marriage to a complete stranger.

The belief that women are of no value is not only held within some societies, but also in some churches. There are places where women are required to be silent and sit in a separate area from the men. They are not allowed to hold any position of leadership where they would need to give instructions to men.

When it comes to industry, some of the most valuable contributions, made by women, have been dismissed because they are believed to be coming from an unreliable 'emotional' source.

Not only is a woman considered inferior in many circles, it has also been inferred that she's a complicated machine whose wiring is impossible to understand. People prefer to relate to her based on their prejudices, ingrained social values, misconceptions, and worldly experiences. As a result, they forfeit the blessing she brings. They never get to enjoy the heavenly fragrance and beauty that God intended her to release because they never consult Him about issues relating to her – yet He is the One who really knows and understands her. Instead, their preconceived ideas cause them to underestimate her and mistreat or even abuse her.

Over the years that I have been involved in women's ministry, I've come to realise that there is something worse than a woman being treated badly because of the environment she lives in, and that is a woman who actually believes she is worthless. This woman is likely to settle for an average life, because she doesn't realise her potential. She may even end up wandering aimlessly through life, becoming a prophetic fulfilment of what the world says about her. Yet this is not God's original intention for her.

There is a principle that is used when studying Bible Interpretation which establishes how God originally intended things to be from the beginning. It's called the 'first mention principle'. When you are looking for answers for origins of a concept in a particular matter, you find where it is first mentioned in the Bible.

The word 'woman' or 'female' is first mentioned in *Genesis 1:27*, *'So God created man in His own image, in the image and likeness of God He created him; male and female He created them'* (Amplified version). From this scripture we see that God created a woman in His own image and likeness. She was to resemble Him and be a representation of Him. God wanted a woman to be just like Him – not inferior to anything or anyone. This is part of God's original intention for a woman.

The Bible goes on to say in *Genesis 1:31* that *'God saw everything that He had made, and behold, it was very good (suitable, pleasant) and He approved it completely...'* (Amplified version). In the original Hebrew text, the word 'good' (*tobe*) can also be defined as pleasant, agreeable, excellent, rich, valuable in estimation, appropriate and becoming. This is what God created a woman to be and there is nothing negative or bad about her. Everything God does is good (*James 1:17*) because He is good (*Psalm 106:1*).

Now let's take a look at how a woman was formed. *Genesis 2:21–22* says, *'And the Lord God caused a deep sleep to fall on Adam, and he slept; and He took one of his ribs, and closed up the flesh in its place. Then the rib which the Lord God had taken from man He made into a woman, and He brought her to the man.'*

A woman's formation was completely different from the rest of God's creation. God didn't form her from the dust of the ground, as He did with Adam. Instead He caused a deep sleep to fall on Adam, took out one of his ribs, and created Eve (Hebrew meaning 'Chavvah' – life giver). God formed her from His already finished product, Adam. When she was introduced to Adam, she was a fully formed and mature woman. God didn't make a baby girl out of Adam's rib and present her to him. No, He made an adult who was ready for her mission in life. He made her complete, whole and beautiful.

Eve was pure, without any blemish and sinless. How do we know this? Because God does not dwell where sin is (*1 John 3:5*). Eve's formation took place in an environment of absolute holiness and as a result, she radiated God's glory (*Isaiah 43:7*). She was an embodiment of both inner and outer beauty and she contained an original, exquisite fragrance that permeated everywhere.

Adam was greatly mesmerised when he first laid eyes on Eve. He had never seen anything like her before. Even though some of her features were similar to his, Eve was totally different. There was nothing on earth like her. Adam was ecstatic to receive Eve, God's amazing masterpiece. His first sight of her even made him poetic when he declared, *'This is now bone of my bones and flesh of my flesh...' (Genesis 2:23).*

By the time Eve was introduced, Adam had already finished naming all the living creatures (take a look at *Genesis 2:19–20*) and when it came to giving Eve a name, he didn't call her something like 'zebra... giraffe... hippopotamus... elephant...' Instead *'Adam called his wife's name Eve, because she was the mother of all living' (Genesis 3:20).*

The way Adam named Eve was distinct from the rest of God's creation. Adam said, *'...she shall be called Woman, because she was taken out of Man' (Genesis 2:23).* She was taken out of him, whilst the rest of God's creation did not come out of Adam and that made her special and unique.

From the beginning, God's intention for a woman has not changed to this present day. What God purposed from the beginning still stands. Although the world and its ideas have changed, God has not changed.

His original plan for a woman remains intact. The world will always try to shape a woman into what it believes she should be, instead of empowering her to be everything God intends her to be. And sadly, if a woman doesn't know what God's Word says concerning her life, she may allow the world's view to shape her. She may never rise up to be all that God destined for her to be. She may never release her heavenly fragrance to bless the world around her.

Woman, God's intention for you has never changed. What He purposed from the beginning still stands. You don't have to wait for anyone to give you permission to become everything that God desires you to be – you already have *His* permission, and that's all you need. The first thing you need to do, though, is to decide from today that you will believe God's Word over everyone else's. You need to choose to see yourself the way God sees you – valuable, special and totally unique. Let God's Word become the greatest influence and authority in your life.

I want to encourage you that it's not where you *are* that counts, but where you are *going*. It's not how you started, but how you finish. You were born with successful genes and your background doesn't have to keep you in the background! Don't allow anyone to redefine you and to squeeze you into their own mold. Don't allow the world and it's views to shape you. Determine from today to be everything that God created you to be. You are significant because the significant One made you in His image and that original, magnificent fragrance still resides in you. It's just waiting to be released!

FRAGRANCE POINTS

1. It is not the world's definition of a woman that counts, but God's definition.

2. A woman was created in the image and likeness of God. She is therefore not inferior to anything or anyone.

3. A woman can become everything that God created her to be when she decides to believe His Word over everyone else's.

'It is time for women of Biblical faith to reclaim our territory. We know the Designer. We have His instruction manual. If we don't display the Divine design of His female creation, no one will. But if we do, it will be a profound testimony to a watching, needy world.' Susan Hunt

---

CHAPTER TWO

What happened to the fragrance?

When I was potty training Lebo, my second child, I noticed how conscious she was of not making a mess in her panties because now she was a 'big girl'! One day we were socialising with some friends, having fun, when all of a sudden we became aware of a funny smell in the atmosphere. We noticed over time that the smell wasn't going anywhere. It just seemed to be lingering and getting worse and, in fact, it was quite offensive.

I asked my daughter, 'Lebo, did you do anything?' She said, 'I think I've just made a bubble,' which meant she had passed some wind, but this one was persisting. All of us were now beginning to feel a little uncomfortable and disturbed by this 'bubble' and I kept thinking, 'What type of a bubble is this?'

Eventually I said to Lebo, 'Let's go and check.' When we got to the toilet we discovered that the 'bubble' was actually quite a big poo! Lebo began to cry. She felt so bad and was embarrassed. It seemed as though the world had crashed on her shoulders and she didn't know what I was going to do about it. She couldn't clean herself up and she stood there helplessly. This one incident disrupted the flow of her day. She had been joyful and vibrant with lots of energy but now everything stood still. She was stuck in a mess she couldn't clean.

I felt compassion for her so I came to her rescue. I cleaned her mess and changed her. My love for her went beyond the smell and mess. I taught her that next time she thought it was just a 'bubble' it would be best to check because some 'bubbles' can quickly turn into something more. After our brief training session Lebo went out again without shame, continuing where she had left off – having fun and enjoying her day!

Like Lebo's incident, many women experience things in their lives that start off as an insignificant bubble that they hope will simply fade away without being noticed. But the bubble persists and becomes an offensive smell which hovers around them, causing everyone else to block their noses each time they come into contact with them. The dilemma of such women is that they don't know how to get rid of this offensive odour. Indeed some are not even aware of it – like having bad breath that everyone, apart from the owner, can smell.

Often, those who are aware of the bad odour don't have the courage to try and help. Sometimes they gossip or even laugh about it. Wanting to be accepted, the woman in this quandary tries to cover up the odour. The attempts women make to 'cover up' are not new. They can be traced back to the Garden of Eden where Adam and Eve tried to cover themselves up after they had sinned.

God had given an instruction that they should not eat from the tree of the knowledge of good and evil, but Eve *'took of its fruit and ate. She also gave to her husband with her, and he ate' (Genesis 3:6)*. As soon as Adam and Eve ate, they were spiritually separated from God. They now realised that they were naked and, in an attempt to cover up, they sewed fig leaves together to cover their nakedness.

Adam and Eve were so ashamed for what they had done that they hid amongst the trees in the garden. God saw everything that happened, because nothing was hidden from His sight, and yet He still came looking for them asking 'Where are you? ... What have you done?' *(Genesis 3:9).*

What Adam and Eve did was no surprise to God because He knew what they had done, but He loved them so much He came to their rescue. God knew they couldn't save themselves, so His solution for covering Adam and Eve's nakedness was to shed the blood of an animal and cover them with skin. It was a far more effective solution than fig leaves and was also a symbol of things to come – a representation of Jesus Christ, whose blood was shed for all of mankind's sin.

Adam and Eve must have been devastated when they realised that their disobedience to God's instruction didn't produce the desired results assured by the devil (*Genesis 3:5*). Eve, instead of attaining the illusion of what she thought she could be, lost the reality of the perfect life she had initially enjoyed – sweet and unhindered fellowship with God. In doing so, she lost her beautiful fragrance.

As it was in Eve's case, many women today try to cover up the sin in their lives with 'fig leaves' such as make-up, designer-branded clothing, fancy cars, ambitious careers, beautiful houses, and being seen with the 'right' social crowd. Looking good on the outside is more important to them than looking good on the inside.

Other women may use these types of 'fig leaves' to try to cover up pain and shame in their lives, pain caused by experiences they've endured through circumstances which they didn't engineer. Perhaps they were violated by someone they trusted, or maybe a relationship that promised them security and love ended in violence and abuse, robbing them of their dignity and potential, leaving them bound.

Some women are afraid because they can't tell anyone their big secret – they don't want to be stigmatised. Sometimes the terrible things that happened were within the confines of their own family, and breaking the silence would be seen as a betrayal of trust or being disloyal. This leaves them feeling isolated and totally helpless.

In their quest to find help, many women hide behind things like illicit sex, drugs, alcohol, work, having overactive social lives, going to party after party or clubbing incessantly, or anything else which serves as a painkiller for their hurting lives. They don't know how to deal with their situation so they put a bandage on their heart. Their pain is covered up, but it's not being treated.

These women become bitter and hardened, hollow instead of being whole. To the outside world everything looks fine, but sooner or later their bitterness becomes like a cancer which begins to destroy them from the inside causing a putrefaction of the original fragrance created by God to emanate from them. Something happened that disrupted the course of their lives. They started well, then an event took place and they got stuck, unable to move on.

Ecclesiastes 10:1 says, '*Dead flies putrefy the perfumer's ointment, and cause it to give off a foul odour; so does a little folly to one respected for wisdom and honour.'* 'Dead flies' or 'flies of death' are likened to the various experiences many women have been through. Unless these 'dead flies' are removed, it's only a matter of time before they begin to give off an offensive odour and the perfume becomes contaminated and the fragrance is polluted.

Some specific examples of 'dead flies' might be:

- betrayal, rejection, adultery, divorce
- racial discrimination, prejudice
- growing up in poverty or with lack
- being raised by cruel step-parents
- loss of virginity, abortion, miscarriage, stillbirth
- depression due to failure to cope with problems
- circumstances that have forced one to become a single parent
- sexual, physical, emotional and/or mental abuse by a family member, friend, employer or any other person
- being forced into an arranged marriage which is not working and feeling 'stuck' there
- exposure to occult practices or witchcraft and not knowing how to get out of their control
- contraction of HIV or a sexually transmitted disease (STD) through infidelity of a spouse

Perhaps you have experienced some of these, or other, 'dead flies'. It's quite possible that I haven't mentioned something you have experienced, but that's only because the list is endless. What you need to know is that the results or effects are the same. No matter how big or small your experience has been, be encouraged, God saw everything that happened to you as well as everything that you did. God doesn't look at the size of your experience, He simply sees you as an individual and understands what you've been through.

Just as it was in the case of my daughter Lebo and her 'bubble', to someone else it may have looked like something trivial but, in her mind, her whole little world was falling apart. To someone else, what you have been through may seem like a small thing, but to you it may seem as if your whole world has fallen to pieces. Although not everyone will be able to identify with you or understand what you've been through, the good thing is that God does.

You may question why God didn't intervene in your situation or stop what was happening to you. The fact is that God may have intervened and saved you from something worse happening to you. You just didn't realise it. And remember that God gave human beings a free will. Your situation may have arisen from a decision which either you or someone else made. Be assured, however, that God would never engineer circumstances to hurt you, so don't reduce Him to your level of understanding and blame Him.

Don't blame God for your pain. He is, in fact, the very One who will set you free. Blaming Him will keep you in a place of bondage. What you need to do is offer all the broken pieces of your life to Him because He is the only one who can put them all back together again, and in the right order. After all, He is the One who formed and fashioned you in your mother's womb, so He knows how to help you. If something is broken, who better to get to fix it than the designer and manufacturer?

You were formed by God. Your life began in His presence. The fact that you are breathing and your heart is beating means there is hope for you and your situation. You may not be aware of it, but He has been carrying you and God never wastes any of our experiences.

When some perfumes are made, petals, flowers, sweet spices or fruits are crushed and mixed with oils. Seeds, twigs, cassia, myrrh, aloes and frankincense, as well as other bitter ingredients, are also mixed together with the sweet ingredients. All the raw ingredients then go through a distillation process of cleansing, decontamination and refining. Out of both sweet and bitter components comes a beautiful fragrance.

In the same way, when all the sweet and bitter components of your life are placed in the hands of the Almighty God, a special, unique and valuable blend of perfume is made. It is important therefore that you don't despise the things you have been through. God can take everything that was crushed and broken in your life and turn it into a stunning fragrance, to be used for His glory.

Isaiah 60:1 declares, *'Arise [from the depression and prostration in which circumstances have kept you – rise to a new life]! Shine (be radiant with the glory of the Lord), for your light has come, and the glory of the Lord has risen upon you!'* (Amplified Version). The 'glory' of the Lord also means His 'ability'. So this scripture is saying that the ability of God has come. The ability to do what? The ability to get you out of your situation because, on your own, you can't. God is willing to lift you up out of the depression, disappointment, discouragement, despair, helplessness, loneliness, guilt, shame, fear, rejection and pain.

The verse also says that you should arise *'from the prostration in which circumstances have kept you'*. Prostrate means lying face down; physically and emotionally exhausted; utterly defeated; thrown down flat; incapacitated in total exhaustion; made weak;

worn out. It can also mean bowing down in an act of worship.

Is this how your experiences have left you feeling? As long as you are still bound by your experiences, you are lying prostrate before them – exhausted, defeated and weak. But God's Word tells you to rise up, He will lift you up. The time we should be prostrate is in worship and thanksgiving before God, not because we are bound by our experiences. Don't allow yourself to be forced into hopelessly lying face down before them. Relocate! Migrate to a better place. It's time to let go of the past.

Lot's wife couldn't let go of the past, even when God tried to rescue her from Sodom, a city that was destructive, immoral and corrupt. Even the angels' attempt to rescue her was not successful, not because they couldn't rescue her, but because she chose to hang on. *Genesis 19:26* says, *'But his [Lot's] wife looked back behind him, and she became a pillar of salt.'* She was so tangled up in her past that she couldn't help looking back on the city that was being destroyed and as a result she was crystallised into a pillar of salt. Her future was instantly killed and all we ever hear about that woman are warnings not to be like her.

Don't sabotage your future because of your past. You need to decide that you want to move on with your life. I'm not suggesting that you deny the things that have happened in your life. On the contrary, you need to acknowledge them, but don't be crystallised by them. Life must continue but as long as you are bound by your experiences and focused on the problem you are facing, you will not make any progress.

Ecclesiastes 1:9 says, *'That which has been is what will be, that which is done is what will be done, and there is nothing new under the sun.'* Realise that you are not the first person to ever be in your situation and if others have been able to move on with their lives with God's help, so can you. Don't allow your circumstances to define who you are. You are not your circumstances. Circumstances change and everything in our lives is subject to change with every decision we make. I encourage you to make a wise decision and move on with your life.

If you are struggling to move on get some help – talk to someone who will have positive input into your life. We are told in *Proverbs 12:25* that, *'Anxiety in the heart of man causes depression, but a good word makes it glad.'* Don't go to someone who will endorse the problem you are facing or simply sympathise with you without helping you find a solution. Go to a person from whom you know you will receive that 'good word'.

I know you may want to isolate yourself and probably don't feel like discussing your problem with anyone, but the fact that you have this book in your hands means the Lord wants to help you. The question is, 'Are you going to say yes to God's help?'

We have all gone through hardship, but there is hope. Jesus can help because He has been victorious in the worst of all circumstances. He was betrayed, denied, rejected, scourged, spat on, unjustly tried and eventually crucified. And yet He chose to forgive the people who subjected Him to tremendous pain. Thank God He rose again and now He qualifies to help because He identifies with our pain.

God says to you, *'Call to Me, and I will answer you...' (Jeremiah 33:3)*. The Lord says, 'Talk to me because I made you. I am willing and able to help you. Before you went through what you went through I was there. When you go through what you go through I am there. And after you have been through it I will still be there. You can trust Me. I won't let you down, even if you are blaming Me for all these things that have happened to you' (Read *Isaiah 43:1-2)*.

Isaiah 61:7 promises, *'Instead of your shame you shall have double honor, and instead of confusion they shall rejoice in their portion. Therefore in their land they shall possess double; everlasting joy shall be theirs.'* God wants to clothe you with honour, dignity and beauty. He wants to heal you, restore you and make you whole again. God promises you double honour for all your shame.

God is an amazing restorer and He will restore everything that the enemy has taken from you. In *Joel 2:25–27* God's promise is, *'So I will restore to you the years that the swarming locust has eaten, the crawling locust, the consuming locust, and the chewing locust, My great army which I sent among you. You shall eat in plenty and be satisfied, and praise the name of the Lord your God, who has dealt wondrously with you; and My people shall never be put to shame. Then you shall know that I am in the midst of Israel: I am the Lord your God and there is no other. My people shall never be put to shame.'*

God will also use your story – the beautiful fragrance of your life – to minister to someone else. When your fragrance is released and you come into contact with others and share how God brought you through, your life will be a true aroma that blesses the lives of those around you. He will use what you've been through to give hope to a hopeless person, to someone else who feels that they are in a pit, so that they too may be free to walk and leap. You will be able to encourage others to rise to their original height instead of staying bruised, broken and crushed.

God will replace your former putrid, decaying and foul odour with a fresh, clean, pure and beautiful fragrance. Someone, somewhere, is waiting for *you* to be made whole. They are waiting to be blessed by the fragrance of your story as you tell them how the Creator has transformed your ashes into beauty.

Lastly, in *2 Corinthians 2:14* the Bible says, *'Now thanks be to God who always leads us in triumph in Christ, and through us diffuses the fragrance of His knowledge in every place.'* When you give your life and all your brokenness to Christ, He will put all the pieces together again and you will diffuse the fragrance of His knowledge everywhere you go. The knowledge of what? The knowledge of His restoration and transforming power that has healed you and changed your life! And that's a beautiful fragrance.

FRAGRANCE POINTS

1. Place your life in God's hands. You can trust Him. He is willing and able to make you whole.

2. Every bitter and sweet experience of your life can be used by God to produce a beautiful fragrance.

3. Your fragrance is for the benefit of others.

'When somebody bruises and hurts you, be like a violet, which gives fragrance to those who step on it. They end up smelling better than their deed.' (Author unknown)

My prayer is that we be so Christlike that we dispense His fragrance, even to those who try to crush us.

CHAPTER THREE

The fragrance of a suitable helper

'I, Fatima Chimkupete, take you, Osien Sibanda, to be my lawfully wedded husband, to have and to hold, for better, for worse, for richer, for poorer, in sickness and in health, to love and to cherish; from this day forward until death do us part. And hereto I pledge to you my faithfulness.'

That was it! I made my vow and it was official. I was now a wife.

Osie and I began our marriage with those amazing promises to cherish one another, no matter what. Our wedding day was very exciting. People came from different places to celebrate with us. We enjoyed the food, the music and the dancing. Little did I know that you don't become a happily married wife just because you have made wedding vows. I had no clue what it meant to live out those vows before God and man, but I was soon going to find out!

We went on our honeymoon and all seemed very pretty and flowery. Even though the honeymoon had its own challenges, we were still living in fantasyland. The euphoria ended once we came home and began living together as husband and wife. We became aware of the differences in our backgrounds, especially in the way we'd been raised. We had not received any premarital counselling at all and the only reference I had of a married man was my father, who is a very loving man.

When my sisters and I were growing up my dad would polish our shoes, do the ironing and general housework and when we didn't feel well he would tenderly and patiently nurse us back to health. Having worked as a cook, he made a variety of meals using numerous spices. He even grew mint in our garden so he could use it when he was preparing meatballs. He would stuff and roast anything from chicken to rabbit and we enjoyed dishes like his homemade meat pies and mincemeat.

Breakfast in our household would often be full English: bacon, eggs, sausages, baked beans, tomato, and mushrooms. After cooking all these delicious meals, he would tidy up to the point that you couldn't tell he'd been working on the stove.

So there I was, a newlywed, dreaming that my husband was going to cook me breakfast and roast dinners, that he would iron and keep the house tidy and that we would work together as a great team. Then bang! The first clash came when I asked him to go and buy food for breakfast. To my utter amazement Osie came back with bread and butter. When I asked him where the breakfast things were, he said, 'Can't you see them? What do you mean?' At first I thought it was a big joke, but after a while I realised he meant it – for him that was breakfast!

Dinner was no different. I could make roast potatoes for dinner and he would say that they were just the relish, where was the pap (thick maize meal porridge)? He also told me that green salad was for grazing cows, and did I expect him to eat uncooked vegetables?!?

And there were other differences… Osie came from a culture where it was shameful for a man to be found in the kitchen, so when his friends came to visit he would run away, leaving me in there to work alone! I also found it hard to believe that he would leave his bath towel on the floor, he would never close the toothpaste tube or replace lotion tops and would forget to clean the bathtub when he had finished bathing. It was a complete shock to my system. Because my dad was the first man in my life, my expectation was that every man would be like him. This may seem trivial, but believe me it caused a lot of tension. I soon discovered that my husband was the total opposite of my dad in every way!

To top it all, financial difficulties arose. I discovered that Osie had gone into partnership with some of his friends, using some of the money we had received as a wedding gift. He bought Jersey dairy cows with the intention of selling the milk. He started this project two months into our marriage and was rarely at home because he was busy on a farm, miles away. To my sheer frustration, his friends would collect him early in the morning and drop him home late in the evening, sometimes as late as midnight. As you can imagine, I felt very lonely and spent much of my time in tears, missing none other than my dad! I wanted to go home. I felt trapped in the 'for worse' part of my vows.

I thought things couldn't deteriorate any further, but then the Jersey cows contracted a disease and even more of the little money we had was being poured into providing medication for them. What was meant to be a business venture to help us out financially was now tearing us apart. Resentment began to settle in my heart, so I cried out to God for help… and the cows began dying, one by one!

I couldn't see a way out of this situation so I took it upon myself to confront the men Osie was working with. In Osie's culture it was considered offensive for a woman to confront a man, so to them this was way out of line and I became a disgrace in their sight. From my point of view, though, they didn't seem to grasp how hard it was for me – they and their wives were all much older than my husband and I, and they all had children. So while they were out gallivanting with my man, I was stuck at home, a new bride, all alone. Osie was seeing in me a spoilt little girl and I was seeing in him a backward man. We were perishing. We had no counsel and I felt I couldn't confess my feelings and struggles to anyone.

Many people had prophesied that our marriage would fail and I didn't want to contribute to the fulfilment of those prophecies, even though I was tempted to get right out of the vows I had made just a few months earlier! Thank God He heard my cry. The Lord sent me help just in time and directed me, through some friends, to an interdenominational women's organisation – Gracious Women Fellowship International. With the help of the mature mothers in this organisation who walked with me, things began to change. They coached me and taught me how to love my husband.

Like many newlyweds, I did not release a sweet fragrance into my marriage. I was a bitter woman – complaining and critical – because things were not being done my way and I was not willing to change. I desperately wanted to change my husband into someone who would be more like my dad. His failure to perform according to my standards caused me to be prickly. It's no wonder he chose to be with his friends! My attitude was driving him away from me and towards them, while I was blaming him.

Without being aware of it, I was releasing an offensive odour that choked him. When I joined Gracious Women, they showed me the godly perspective of a wife and taught me to how to apply Biblical principles in my marriage.

In *Genesis 2:18* it says, *'And the Lord God said, "It is not good that man should be alone; I will make him a helper comparable to him."'* It was not Adam who brought a prayer request to God asking for a wife. God saw it was not good for man to be alone, so He formed Eve for a specific purpose which could not be fulfilled by any of His other creation already in existence. Out of all the birds, animals and living creatures *'there was not found a helper comparable to him' (Genesis 2:20).* Eve was God's solution. She was created to facilitate fruitfulness, multiplication and companionship in Adam's life, to help him be a faithful steward of God's creation and to have dominion.

Together with Adam they would enjoy fellowship with the Lord and be productive on the earth. They were the pioneers of the human race and pioneers of marriage, and their marriage was good. Eve was good for Adam, she was his companion and wife.

A wife comes alongside her husband to help him, just as Eve came alongside Adam to help him. The Hebrew word for help is 'ezer', meaning 'suitable helper' or 'help meet'. That means she aids and helps. Adam wouldn't have been able to reach his potential without his wife's help. She was the right type, or quality, for that purpose and she was appropriate for him.

There is a beautiful description of a wife in the *Song of Songs 4:12-16* that says, *'My sweetheart, my bride, is a secret garden, a walled garden, a private spring; there the plants flourish. They grow like an orchard of pomegranate trees and bear the finest fruits. There is no lack of henna and nard, of saffron, calamus, and cinnamon, or incense of every kind. Myrrh and aloes grow there with all the most fragrant perfumes. Fountains water the garden, streams of flowing water, brooks gushing down from the Lebanon Mountains. Wake up, North Wind. South Wind, blow on my garden; fill the air with fragrance. Let my lover come to his garden and eat the best of its fruits'* (Good News Bible).

A wife is being compared to this lovely sight of a garden. This garden is enclosed; it's not exposed to everyone. It's protected, secure and reserved for the owner. The marriage covenant separates a woman and she becomes enclosed only for her husband.

A garden is also a place of production. It's a life-giving place where vegetables, fruits and flowers are grown. Things that are produced in a garden refresh and sustain life. Gardens have a sweet fragrance, a smell of freshness, a sense of life and purpose. So is this wife being described in this scripture.

She is also compared to beautiful spices like spikenard (nard), calamus, frankincense, myrrh and aloes, with all the chief spices. Spices are very valuable and bring flavour to food. Spices were also used to embalm and prevent dead bodies from rotting. Even after the birth of Jesus we read that wise men brought gifts to Him – frankincense and myrrh were part of them *(Matthew 2:11).*

In *John 12:3-7* we read about a woman who used spikenard, which is a fragrant oil that produces a strong fragrance. No wonder the Bible says that the fragrance filled the whole house. There was not one part of this house that was not affected by this fragrance.

Myrrh is found on a shrub tree. It's smooth and bitter, acting as an antiseptic and stimulant. It also produces a beautiful and valuable fragrance. Henna, calamus, saffron and aloe all have medicinal properties and each produce a unique fragrance. All these spices refresh and preserve. This woman in *Song of Songs* is being compared to these valuable spices, suggesting that she preserves and refreshes her marriage. She is a breath of fresh air and she releases a rejuvenating fragrance in her marriage. She is also compared to a fountain of living waters. Water cleanses and purifies and it's of great value to our bodies. No one can survive without it.

This woman knows her purpose in her marriage. She tells the wind to come and blow upon her garden so that her fragrance and spices may flow out. She knows her ministry and calling to her husband is to help him, and when he is wounded to be like the antiseptic to bring restoration, healing and comfort. She has an inner beauty to give out. She is not like a garden that has a rocky ground. Neither does she produce thorns and briars, making it difficult to plant in the garden.

God's plan for a wife has not changed. He desires her to be valuable and precious to her husband; to have a sweet and loving spirit and to belong only to him. Together He purposed that they would be fruitful and multiply in every area of their lives so that He may be glorified. However, this is a process because a wife is not born already suitable, looking like this lovely garden as described. She becomes suitable as she grows and lives together with her husband in marriage, as they begin to merge, adjust and adapt to their new life. It takes a willing heart, wisdom, patience and the ability to learn from others to become a relevant and suitable wife.

There are different principles that can help you to become a suitable helper to your husband like that lovely garden. You could use some of these principles in your marriage. If you're not married, you could use these principles in the future. Let's take a look at them.

FRAGRANT COMFORTER

When the Jersey cows from my husband's new business venture were sick and dying, I definitely wasn't a comfort to him. I wasn't like that myrrh that works like an antiseptic to bring healing and to sooth his pain. I was ill-equipped to handle the situation and in my ignorance I rubbed salt into his wounds. To be truthful, I really wanted those cows to die – they were my enemies, competing for my husband's attention.

Looking back, had I prayed for them to live, maybe we would both have benefited from the business. Certainly it would have been much more helpful if I'd had a positive attitude about it. I could have encouraged my husband, comforted him and prayed for him – but at the time I knew only how to pour very cold water on his ideas, determined to hinder him. The problem was that I didn't really understand my mission as a wife. Believe it or not, all I dreamt of when I got married was a beautiful wedding dress and a cake with a fountain, because that was the fashion at the time.

In life, things do not always turn out the way we plan them. Husbands may fail to meet their goals and targets at work, in the ministry or at home. Some may not be where they thought they would be at a particular stage in their life. Perhaps they made bad decisions that hindered their progress. That is not the time to sing the 'I told you so' song or to recite the 'you should have listened to me' poem. Rather, encourage your husband during times of difficulty and weakness.

Let a comforting fragrance flow out of you by being sensitive to your husband and his miscalculations. Stand by him, minister to him, and bring in a godly perspective to reignite the hope in his heart. Analyse his situation and don't speak hastily. Determine in your heart to become a comforting fragrance. Be like that refreshing fountain of water.

FRAGRANCE YOUR WORDS

When talking to your husband *'let no corrupt word proceed out of your mouth, but what is good for necessary edification, that it may impart grace...'* (Ephesians 4:29).

Always use wisdom, tact and discretion. Wisdom helps you to know what to say, tact is working out how to say it and discretion is recognising when to say it. *Proverbs 31:26* describes a wise woman as one who *'opens her mouth with wisdom, and on her tongue is the law of kindness.'* Such a woman releases fragrant words. She doesn't use her words as weapons.

When I look back I realise that when I confronted Osie's friends and business partners about their Jersey cow venture, I didn't use any wise words. I went to challenge men I felt were being very selfish and were out to destroy my marriage while they were enjoying theirs. I accused them of taking my husband away from me and not caring about us, even though they were elders in the church! I didn't care about their age or position because I was bent on destroying their relationship with my husband. I even accused them of not wanting to spend time with their own wives!

I told them to stop coming early in the morning to fetch Osie, to refrain from interfering with our marriage, and I even told their wives to keep their husbands to themselves. I did not use pleasant words to address this. Osie's heart began to harden towards me because his friends accused him of being ruled by a woman from another tribe. There was no law of kindness on my tongue, only a law of ruthlessness. I realise now that I should have approached those men prayerfully, with a meek spirit and the right attitude. Before we got married they were already an integral part of Osie's life and I had just arrived on the scene. I should have asked God to provide a strategy to wean him from those relationships.

Solomon, recognised as the wisest man in the Bible, said in *Proverbs 18:21*, *'death and life are in the power of the tongue, and those who love it will eat its fruit.'* You can speak fragrant, life-giving words to your husband or you can release poisonous words that will destroy him.

In the book of James, the Bible once again stresses the importance of how you use your tongue. *'And the tongue is a fire, a world of iniquity. The tongue is so set among our members that it defiles the whole body, and sets on fire the course of nature; and it is set on fire by hell' (James 3:6)*. Does your husband live in a world of iniquity created by your tongue? Does he receive both sweet and bitter water from your mouth? *James 3:8-11* goes on to say, *'But no man can tame the tongue. It is an unruly evil, full of deadly poison. With it we bless our God and Father, and with it we curse men, who have been made in the similitude of God. Out of the same mouth proceed blessing and cursing. My brethren, these things ought not to be so. Does a spring send forth fresh water and bitter from the same opening?'*

Do you respect your husband with your words or do you make him feel insecure? Do you compare him to other men like I compared Osie to my father? I would sometimes say to him, 'My father could have cleaned the bathtub and not spilled water everywhere' or 'he could have washed his socks, not like you!' But then when Osie did something good I would speak words of praise to him, especially if he led worship or preached well according to my standards. I was giving him both bitter and sweet water from the same mouth. So when I wasn't happy Osie lived in a world of iniquity, but then in a fragrant, refreshing world when I was happy with him. You shouldn't do things like this.

My late mum always quoted *Proverbs 14:1* to me, *'The wise woman builds her house, but the foolish pulls it down with her hands.'* She often reminded me how a foolish woman can destroy her home with her words, pulling it down, while a wise woman builds her home. You can easily destroy your home with words, so be a wise woman who speaks words of wisdom. Know when to speak and when to be quiet; when to joke and when to be serious. Don't be the one who trashes his ideas when everyone else is celebrating them. He'll want to be around those who appreciate his presence.

Avoid becoming an ally, friend or associate of anyone who speaks badly about your husband, even if what they are saying is right. Defend him publicly, then lovingly and prayerfully confront the situation at the right time with a sweet spirit, showing him honour and respect. That way, he will be open to your counsel and listen to what you have to say.

Don't counsel or advise your husband in a way that manipulates him to do what you want, nor endorse that which is ungodly. Whatever counsel you give, it must be in line with the Word of God. Every time you open your mouth to speak to your husband, let it be sweet like the sweet spices which produce a godly fragrance.

FRAGRANCE OF UNDERSTANDING

Proverbs 4:7 states, *'in all your getting, get understanding.'* An understanding wife is like a breath of fresh air to her husband. You need to understand your husband in order to be a suitable helper. How can you help a person you don't understand? Who will you really be helping?

Study your husband quietly. Observe the things he does and how he functions. The more you seek to understand your husband, the less conflict you will have and the more you will enjoy your marriage.

There are many things that can help you understand your husband better, here are some:

- Prayer – ask the Lord to give you understanding and show you what you need to know
- Find out what is it that makes him feel loved
- Be aware of his background or culture – you don't have to make it your own, but it can help you understand why he does things the way he does
- Understanding his spirituality – observe his devotional life, involvement in church, his giftings and calling, his relationships – and find ways to encourage him
- Ask him questions when you are unsure about why he does the things he does

I am still learning to understand my husband, but in some things I understand him very well because I've learnt to ask the necessary questions to give me insight into how he thinks and sees life. For example, Osie's family never placed great importance on remembering birthdays or special occasions like anniversaries, whereas my family is the complete opposite. So when it came to my birthday or my family's birthdays I would remind him of the date. Instead of setting myself up for disappointment, I learnt to help my husband remember.

You can remind your husband about your birthday. Don't spend all night crying because he's forgotten to buy you a card. Remember it's *your* birthday, not his. If he tends to be the type who forgets things, you could remind him of some of the following: commitments he's made; important dates; your children's activities at school; church events; bills which need to be paid; where his socks, tie, wallet, keys and mobile phone are. Don't accuse your husband when he's genuinely forgotten something. Remember your husband is human, like you, and he's likely to forget.

There are some husbands who are detail conscious and tend to remember everything. If your husband is one of these then don't nag him because it may seem like you're interfering or being too forward. You may end up upsetting him.

It is possible to release the fragrance of understanding to your husband. Don't allow an offensive odour into your marriage by your lack of understanding, but rather allow your fragrant understanding to refresh your husband.

FRAGRANCE OF SUBMISSION

Being a suitable helper for your husband means learning to submit to him. Although challenging for many women and taken to the extreme by some, submission is a very positive thing when done in the spirit of humility and love. Don't be stubborn and difficult like a wild garden that produces thorns and briars which cannot be cultivated.

In *Ephesians 5:22* it says, *'Wives, submit to your own husbands, as to the Lord.'* Submission involves yielding yourself to your husband's love which includes taking correction, submitting to his decisions, and trusting and accepting his leadership. It's ultimately trusting God with him. This doesn't mean that you don't question or discuss issues, but the spirit in which you question shouldn't be undermining, trying to usurp his authority or compete with him.

When you submit to your husband, you are desiring what's best for both of you, knowing that ultimately the Lord is in control.

FRAGRANCE OF TRUTH

'And you shall know the truth, and the truth shall make you free' (John 8:32). A fragrant wife is truthful. As a fragrant wife, you should not lie to your husband. How will he really know you if you are not honest and transparent with him about your feelings? Even when you think that telling the truth is going to cost you, still do it – don't fear! If you lie in order to please him your lies will ultimately cost you more. And don't just tell him the truth about yourself, tell him the truth about himself too. If he does something wrong, don't pretend it's okay or agree with him in order to avoid conflict, rather lovingly communicate how you perceive things.

Telling your husband the truth will save you a lot of heartache. There was a couple in the Bible who failed to tell the truth and it ended up costing them their lives. Ananias and Sapphira *(Acts 5:1–10)* failed to tell the truth concerning the sale of their property. Ananias lied first and then Sapphira came and endorsed the lie, and as a result they both died. Had she told the truth, the story would have been different.

I know of a lady who was secretly sending money to her family. In addition she became involved with another man at work. She ran a private telephone line on which she would talk to him, sometimes until very late. Her husband discovered all these things through a bank statement, and sadly that marriage is now history. She failed to tell her husband the truth. If you've been doing 'funny deals' behind your husband's back, don't wait for him to discover them. Telling him the truth, although very difficult, will set you free even though the consequences may be tough.

If you find yourself thinking about other men, or if other men are trying to get too close to you, whether at work or even in ministry, make sure you tell your husband. Don't compromise yourself, or try to justify your behaviour with exaggerations or half-truths. Avoid misleading your husband at all costs.

Ephesians 4:25 says, *'Therefore, putting away lying, "Let each one of you speak truth with his neighbor," for we are members of one another.'* There is nothing as damaging as a devious, lying wife. If you lie to your husband with the intention of deceiving him into believing that things are not what they really are, it shows that you don't value him. Even casual lies must be stopped. They can easily turn into habitual lies. Imagine what would happen if the truth were to be discovered about your lies and what an offensive odour would be released when many, especially your husband, are hurt as a result. It's not worth it. Remain a woman of integrity whom your husband's heart can trust. Release a genuine fragrance, not an imitation.

A WORD OF CAUTION

There is an area of truth that many women try to hide instead of exposing. You should not excuse any violent behaviour from your husband, especially if you are being abused. Don't lie that you had an accident and hit your face against the wall, when your husband is abusing you. Tell your husband that you will not tolerate such behaviour, then go and get help. Don't keep it a secret until it's too late.

Don't allow intimidation to silence you. Don't allow gifts and sweet-talk to cause you to excuse aggressive behaviour. Your silence about it could cause him to abuse you until you are permanently silenced in your coffin. Before that happens, speak to those close to you about it or your spiritual overseers.

If necessary, notify the police for your safety and protection and your husband's, because when he's been confronted by others or by the law, he might change.If you don't get help, the unexpressed anger inside you might end up causing you to do something dangerous which you will regret in your future. Abused wives have been known to burn their husbands with boiling water, or to attack them with a dangerous weapon when least expected. Don't break your silence in a spirit of revenge but in one of needing help.

On the other hand, avoid accusing your husband of abuse just because you don't want to be corrected when you have done something wrong. Be realistic about your situation; don't create a monster out of him. Above all, always pray for your him. God is the only One who can change his heart.

FRAGRANCE AND YOUR IN-LAWS

Ask the Lord to help you appreciate the family your husband came from and to treat them as your own. They are the vessels God chose to produce a husband for you, so honour them. If you treat them badly you are actually despising where he came from. Whether you believe them to be good or bad people, respect them. Don't gossip about them. Learn to minister to their needs and bless them as often as you can, but not at the expense of your children or your marriage.

Don't allow the in-laws on either side to disrupt the harmony in your home. If you feel that certain demands they are making are unreasonable, tell your husband of your concerns openly and honestly. Handle everything with love and prayer so that you can release a sweet fragrance to your in-laws.

FRAGRANT SUPPORT

If your husband is in the ministry, be his greatest supporter. Don't let him be crushed by the pressures of ministry. Watch out for his spiritual, physical and emotional welfare. Don't hinder him. Rather challenge and support him to reach even greater heights.

Whether your husband is in the ministry or works for a company, if he has a personal assistant, use wisdom when dealing with her. Cooperate with her so that you may know your husband's work schedule. This helps avoid clashes between your personal time together and his work or ministry commitments.

Don't change what's in his diary so that you can fill it with yourself. Remember that you are there to support him in his calling. If you are concerned that he is being overbooked with appointments, talk to him at home about it and approach the subject prayerfully.

You shouldn't harass the personal assistant over your husband's diary. She is only doing what she is employed to do. However, if she oversteps the mark or begins to act as though she owns your husband, address the situation wisely. Start by talking to your Heavenly Father about it. Then, having received His wisdom, talk to your husband.

Always check your motives and address issues with a sweet spirit. Don't make your husband change his personal assistant because you have allowed jealousy in your heart. Remember he married *you* so be secure in his love for you.

YOU CAN DO IT!

Go on and release that fragrance. Let a sweet smelling aroma come out of you and fill your husband's life with your love and care. Let your life refresh his. Become the suitable helper that God intended for your husband.

Ask the Lord to help you in the areas of your life that need changing. Determine to be the best wife you can ever be. You can invest in books that will help you improve your marriage and attend any marriage courses or seminars so that you can be empowered.

Let the fragrance of your love for your husband fill your home. Let your marriage be like that lovely garden that is fruitful and productive. Let it be an example for others to follow. Let the single people who observe how you conduct yourself in marriage be encouraged and desire the same for their future. Let your marriage be a blessing to your generation and generations to come so that God may be glorified.

FRAGRANCE POINTS

1. You are your husband's ordained suitable helper.
2. Becoming a relevant wife is a process; it's an amazing journey of discovery.
3. You can release a comforting, understanding, submissive, truthful and supportive fragrance into your husband's life.

'Success in marriage does not come merely through finding the right mate, but through being the right mate.'
Barnett R. Brickner

CHAPTER FOUR

The fragrance of intimacy

One night around midnight, I woke up and went to the toilet. When I came back into our bedroom Osie was nowhere to be seen, yet I had left him in bed. I began to look around for him. I checked in the downstairs toilet, in the children's bedrooms and all the places he might have gone. I even checked in the pantry. I wondered what could have happened to him. I looked through the window; the car was still there, and anyway he wouldn't have gone out in the middle of the night without telling me.

I started saying loudly, 'Where is this man?' I even began praying, 'Lord, where is he?' Then I noticed a coat hanger lying on the floor in our room and thought to myself, 'This is a sharp object, let me put it back in the wardrobe so that no one gets hurt.' When I opened the wardrobe I was still muttering to myself, 'Where is he?' To my complete and utter amazement, there he was, sitting in the wardrobe like a naughty schoolboy, caught by the principal.

'I got you!' he said.

I said, 'Come out of there quickly!' This little episode really made us laugh.

Osie and I have a lot of fun in our marriage and sometimes we live in a world of our own. We can look at each other across a crowded room and communicate without saying a word. Different looks mean different things and we know what they mean.

Whenever Osie enters a room, I can sense him before I see him. He brightens my day. We often share the same opinion about particular situations. It still amazes me when he comes home and says exactly what I've told the children he would say about a certain matter! And when I consult him for wisdom on how to handle a situation, he normally advises me the way I thought he would. We are intimately acquainted with each other's ways. We are the best of friends. He is my greatest supporter and I am his. We love to see each other excelling in every area.

From reading this you may think that Osie and I are a perfect couple with a perfect marriage. By no means are we perfect. Two imperfect people don't make a perfect marriage. We didn't start out this way and to be honest, after a year of being married to him, I didn't think it was going to last. We didn't have the opportunity to receive pre-marriage counselling and, as a result, the foundation that we were trying to build on was very shaky! The storms came and our marriage nearly collapsed.

I cried out to God for help and He connected me, through an interdenominational organisation, with godly women who taught me how to be a good wife to my husband. They taught me how to love him. They taught me how to support, encourage, understand, comfort and minister to him. As my husband began to see changes in me, he also desired to change. He joined the same organisation and through it, God sent him godly men who mentored him. As we both applied the principles we were being taught, our marriage began to blossom and thank God, it's been blossoming ever since.

Having an intimate marriage is not automatic. Every harvest comes from sowing something first. If you want the returns of a happy, blessed and intimate marriage then you need to sow good seeds into it. It takes time and energy. My husband and I have often counselled couples that have been expecting their marriages to flourish automatically without doing anything about it or contributing anything to it.

What we noticed about these couples is that although they were married, they were not intimately involved in each other's lives, they were not friends. Just because two people live in the same house, share the same bed and eat the same food does not mean they are intimately acquainted with each another. They may know a lot about each other, but that does not mean they know each other. For example, he may know she likes eating cereal for breakfast, but is that enhancing their intimacy or is it simply general knowledge about her? She may know he likes watching sports on television, but does that add to their intimacy?

The Message translation of *Psalm 139:1–6* gives a lovely description of intimacy and expresses it beautifully. It says, *'God, investigate my life; get all the facts firsthand. I'm an open book to you; even from a distance, you know what I'm thinking. You know when I leave and when I get back; I'm never out of your sight. You know everything I'm going to say before I start the first sentence. I look behind me and you're there, then up ahead and you're there, too – your reassuring presence, coming and going. This is too much, too wonderful – I can't take it all in!'* Although this scripture speaks about the psalmist's relationship with the Lord, it also applies to intimacy in marriage.

I once heard intimacy described as 'into-me-see'; in other words, allowing someone to know you as you really are; being transparent with them. Intimacy has also been defined as being familiar or very affectionate with someone as a result of having a close and personal relationship. Being intimate with someone is like being an 'open-book', allowing them to freely 'read' you.

Cultivating or maintaining intimacy in marriage is not difficult at all. It's about doing practical things together on a day-to-day basis to affectionately communicate your love and care for one another. There are many things you can do to enhance your intimacy such as going for a walk together, finding special nights where you do things together like watching a wholesome movie, or sending special text messages. You could also take a bath together to wind up your day, if your husband likes that. Plan a romantic candlelight dinner where you cook a very special meal just to appreciate him. You could surprise him with unexpected gifts and no-occasion cards, and send him little love notes in his lunch box if he carries one. You could stick a love message for him on your bedroom mirror. Definitely take advantage of his birthday and your wedding anniversary. It's your opportunity to express your intimacy, love and appreciation for the wonderful gift of a husband that God has given you. Find out what works for you as a couple and what makes him feel special and loved.

Be you husband's best friend. Friendship is one of the greatest tools to develop intimacy because when you are friends, you can communicate anything to each other without fear. Be a safe place for your husband to share his innermost thoughts. He will trust you with the secrets of his heart and your intimacy will deepen as you get closer to each other.

The greatest communication, demonstration and application of oneness in marriage is through sexual intimacy. Jesus endorsed this: *'And He answered and said to them, "Have you not read that He who made them at the beginning 'made them male and female,' and said, 'For this reason a man shall leave his father and mother and be joined to his wife, and the two shall become one flesh'? So then, they are no longer two but one flesh. Therefore what God has joined together, let not man separate"' (Matthew 19:4-6).*

Sexual intimacy is the place where you become one flesh with your husband, with nothing hindering you and nothing coming between you. It's one activity that's tailor-made for the two of you. It's so special and unique to you as a couple, and no one else has a right to be present with you, except for God who is always with you.

The Amplified Bible says in *Hebrews 13:4, 'Let marriage be held in honour (esteemed worthy, precious, of great price, and especially dear) in all things and thus let the marriage bed be undefiled (kept undishonoured); for God will judge and punish the unchaste [all guilty of sexual vice] and adulterous'* (Amplified Version).

God wants you to hold your marriage and the marriage bed in honour, treating it with great respect. The marriage bed is a place where you celebrate the intimacy of your day-to-day life. It's meant to be a safe, special and refreshing sanctuary for you and your husband to rest and be renewed – a place where you minister to and bless your husband with your body;

which belongs to him *(1 Corinthians 7:3–5)*. Don't deny your husband what rightfully belongs to him lest he longs for someone else or resorts to ungodly means to satisfy himself. A husband who is fully satisfied at home will not have a reason wander off. Obviously if he falls into sexual sin he is responsible, but let it not be because you always give selfish excuses such as being tired or having a headache or menstrual pain. This will certainly hinder sexual intimacy. If there are genuine reasons why you can't be sexually intimate with him in bed I am sure he will understand, but always communicate lovingly.

Avoid things that disrupt sexual intimacy like unresolved conflict. Determine to resolve any conflict in your marriage in a godly manner and don't give any place to the devil. Deal with the anger in your heart if your husband has disappointed or let you down, or if he has said something that has bruised and hurt you. *Ephesians 4:26* says, *'"Be angry, and do not sin": do not let the sun go down on your wrath, nor give place to the devil.'*

If you end your day with a 'Cold War', you may wake up facing your enemy and perhaps spend the day in 'World War Three'. Rather resolve to go to bed with a clean heart and the right spirit. It's better to leave whatever burden you are carrying at the foot of cross and *'...submit to God. Resist the devil and he will flee from you' (James 4:7)*. Keep your heart pure because you can't enjoy sexual intimacy with someone you're at war with.

One thing that will unquestionably dishonour God and your husband is sexual immorality. It destroys intimacy and pollutes your marriage. Your sexual needs are supposed to be met within the context of your marriage and not outside. Adultery has devastating effects. When you give your body or your thoughts to another man, you are joining yourself to him when you are only supposed to be joined to your husband. Again, in this day and age, it's very dangerous in that you could contract incurable diseases that you might pass onto your husband and lead to his death, and yours too. I don't think you want to do that. The consequences are more costly than that affair. If you have children, you could now leave them as orphans.

Adultery never begins with the act, it starts with a thought that was entertained and not captured; a thought which was further developed and acted upon. It could have been exposed, repented of and replaced by godly thoughts as those described in

Philippians 4:8 where it says, *'...whatever things are true, whatever things are noble, whatever things are just, whatever things are pure, whatever things are lovely, whatever things are of good report, if there is any virtue and if there is anything praiseworthy – meditate on these things'*. Thinking the right thoughts towards your husband enhances your sexual intimacy. If you want to have great intimacy and fun in bed then you need to be thinking well about your husband all day.

As you continue to develop your intimacy, make sure you communicate truthfully and honestly because, then there is transparency. Truth always frees and empowers. Tell your husband how you want to be handled and ask him how he wants to be handled. Don't fake things in the bedroom. Don't be there bodily while your mind and emotions are elsewhere. If there is anything you are not comfortable with, tell him. If he tells you what he is not comfortable with, don't take offence. Always seek the best for him.

As you communicate, remember the bedroom is not a courtroom where your husband is being tried and you are the judge. It's not a place for solving disputes but a place of celebrating the blessing of your marriage and enjoying your intimate time together.

Remember to keep your special sanctuary clean, inviting and fresh. Don't forget personal hygiene. Always smell good for your man. Change your bed linen often and aerate your bedroom by opening the windows to get rid of any stuffy or bad odours. Release a godly fragrance and a natural fragrance as well!

I want to conclude by reminding you that intimacy is cultivated and developed daily with every investment you make into your marriage. When you give your marriage the honour and respect it deserves, you reap the harvest and blessings of intimacy. God wants you to release a sweet and beautiful fragrance of intimacy in your marriage. Your fragrance can be so good that your husband finds you irresistible, like a perfume that makes a statement you can't ignore; the scent lingers long and lasts all day. Guess what? You can do it!

FRAGRANCE POINTS

1. Having an intimate marriage is not automatic. It takes an investment of time and effort.

2. Be your husband's best friend.

3. Sexual intimacy in marriage is the greatest communication, application and demonstration of oneness.

'Relationships are not for perfect people. Relationships are a means to perfection.' Abraham Sam Aiyedogbon

---

CHAPTER FIVE

The fragrance of a godly mother

One of my sisters is a prison nurse and her job is very challenging. It was not long after she started working in a local prison that she came home one day looking extremely stressed. After a while, she settled down and I asked her what was wrong. She told me that one of the prisoners had committed suicide and another had cut his wrists with a razor blade. She had attended to both incidents that day. It was the first time she had been confronted with such a traumatic situation and it deeply disturbed her. I felt tremendous compassion for my sister and I kept thinking about the prisoner whose life had come to a sudden and tragic end. My thoughts were, 'This was someone's child.'

People are sent to prison for various crimes they have committed. Depending on the gravity of their crime, they are assigned to a specific wing to serve their sentence and are kept away from the rest of society. Others are confined to high security cells away from fellow inmates. They are considered to be capable of committing further crimes, and are sometimes found in possession of dangerous items. This is rather strange because prisoners are not allowed to have such items. How they are able to get hold of them is a wonder in itself!

Offenders were not born this way. Before they were prisoners, they belonged to families and came as a gift from the Lord. The Bible says in *Psalm 127:3–5* that, *'Behold, children are a heritage from the Lord, the fruit of the womb is a reward. Like arrows in the hand of a warrior, so are the children of one's youth. Happy is the man who has his quiver full of them; they shall not be ashamed, but shall speak with their enemies in the gate.'* A heritage infers something good, something that belongs to someone by reason of birth – an inheritance. Children are a heritage from the Lord and are meant to be a blessing. They pass down the norms and values of the family into which they are born from generation to generation.

Children are God's miraculous way of ensuring the continuation of the human race. Just think about the process of conception – it's amazing! What starts out as two merging cells cannot even be compared to the end product of a fully-grown baby, formed by God in the mother's womb. No pregnant woman can claim to have put any parts of her baby together – she simply facilitates its development. She cannot say, 'I put the liver or lungs there' – that fashioning belongs to God. *Psalm 139* says, *'Your eyes saw my substance, being yet unformed' (verse 16)* and, *'...You formed my inward parts; You covered me in my mother's womb' (verse 13).*

The Bible tells us that even the pregnant mother doesn't know how the bones are being formed or the exact day, time and place of their formation – *'As you do not know ... how the bones grow in the womb of her who is with child' (Ecclesiastes 11:5).* Children are formed and created by God in an amazing way. Each one is special and unique. God does the knitting together of every cell to create a human being. The end product of a child is His masterpiece and He graciously allows us to share in the remarkable process of creation.

All children, therefore, have the potential to achieve great things. God, who is no respecter of persons, has ordained them to succeed before the foundation of the world. God doesn't create something in order for it to fail. According to the Lord, children across all races are equal from the time they are conceived in their mother's womb. They are all innocent and pure.

Once a child enters the world, God entrusts the child to his or her parents to create a safe environment to grow and be shaped according to His plan. Even though God's original way was for children to be raised by their own parents in a godly environment, not all children have that privilege. Some children are raised by grandparents or by other guardians due to circumstances beyond their control.

Children become a product of the input of their parents, their environment, as well as their personal choices. This is why parenting is such a great responsibility. Parents are a child's first contact with life, and what is passed on through their training will be imparted into generations to come. *Proverbs 22:6* says that we ought to *'train up a child in the way he should go, and when he is old he will not depart from it.'* We cannot underestimate the power of training. If we don't take the opportunity to train our children in the right way, when they are young, there can be severe consequences. Lack of proper training can lead our children straight into a prison similar to the one where my sister works and, instead of contributing to society, they become a threat to it and a drain on its resources. They end up being locked away because they release a bad odour instead of a godly fragrance which could have benefited society.

Evidently not every child will end up in prison through lack of training or by making bad choices. However, they may end up imprisoned in some areas of their lives and not fulfil the destiny God planned for them. Thank God that He shows us in His Word how to raise children in a godly way. Let's examine some of the characteristics of a fragrant mother and see how to apply them.

A FRAGRANT MOTHER IS A LOVER OF GOD

Deuteronomy 6:4–8 says, *'Hear, O Israel: The Lord our God, the Lord is one! You shall love the Lord your God with all your heart, with all your soul, and with all your strength. And these words which I command you today shall be in your heart. You shall teach them diligently to your children, and shall talk of them when you sit in your house, when you walk by the way, when you lie down, and when you rise up. You shall bind them as a sign on your hand, and they shall be as frontlets between your eyes.'*

A fragrant mother releases a fragrance in her home which stems from her love for the Lord her God. When you love God with all your heart, your fragrance will be like a perfume that fills a room and rubs off onto all those who come into contact with it. The love of God, emanating from you, will spread like a fragrance to your family.

When you love God and minister to Him, He will impart to you the grace you need to raise your children in a godly manner. He will help you to lay down your life for your children and serve your family so that whatever you do, you will *'do it heartily, as to the Lord and not to men' (Colossians 3:23)*. Because you love God, you will minister to your family in obedience to the Lord who says, *'if you love Me, keep My commandments' (John 14:15)*. What are those commandments? To train up your children in the right way.

A FRAGRANT MOTHER IS A GENTLE HELPER

A helper is someone who assists by getting involved. Your children need your involvement in their lives. When they are little, they need you to teach them how to walk, how to feed themselves, how to use the toilet, etc. These are basic life skills which help them grow and take responsibility for their own lives.

Never be so busy with other people or your career that you are not on hand to help them. Don't allow anything to hinder you from being available to help your children or from giving them the support that they need. They want you to be there for them, to have fun with them, to laugh with them, cry with them, celebrate with them – to feel your presence in their lives.

Give them space when they need it but be available for them in every season of their life – when they are young, crying because of a scratched finger; through their teenage years, when they are feeling insecure and looking for identity; to young adulthood, perhaps planning to get married. You need to be available to help your children for as long as they need you. Always be on standby, without necessarily interfering. Being there to help your children is one of the best gifts you can give them.

A FRAGRANT MOTHER GIVES WISE COUNSEL AND PRAYS FOR HER CHILDREN

There is a proverb that says 'Dip your tongue in wisdom, then give counsel.' The wisest counsel comes from the Word of God. When your children have issues they cannot solve or have major decisions to make, give them counsel from God's Word. This is the safest and most effective form of counselling.

It is always wise to take the time to listen to both sides of a story before making judgements or decisions. Don't take everything at face value – you may need to dig deeper by asking lots of questions to get to the truth. If you allow your children to cry for everything that happens, you will raise cry-babies.

Whenever children come crying to me with stories, I tell them to stop crying first so that I can clearly hear what the matter is in order for me to solve the problem. Of course, this doesn't apply when they've physically hurt themselves or are in serious pain. But when the issues are minor, for example, they have argued or fought with a friend, I won't allow tale-telling or foolish crying. I don't want to end up massaging and endorsing their weaknesses.

Rely on the help of the Holy Spirit to reveal to you situations that your children may be facing, so that you can intercede for them. You won't always know what is happening in their daily lives, whether they are at school, university or work, so it's important that you pray for them, their friends, teachers, work colleagues and everyone who is involved in their life.

Not only should you pray *for* your children, pray *with* them as well. Let them hear you pray. Teach and encourage them to pray as well. It's good to demonstrate a healthy prayer life as a role model for them.

A FRAGRANT MOTHER IS AN ENCOURAGER

There will be many times in your children's lives when they will need your encouragement. Often children may come home feeling discouraged – it could be school-related, relationships that aren't working well, even worries over how they look, or they may just have had a bad day. Encourage them. Think about how a bridge is built. For the safety and protection of those who will use it, construction workers build in reinforcements so that it doesn't give way to pressure. As a mother, you can be that strengthener and reinforcer, for your children. You can help them not to give in to pressure, whilst developing their strengths, by being an encouragement to them.

Don't condemn your children for being weak. You are also weak in certain areas of your life. You can encourage your children by sharing with them about times when you have failed and how you overcame that failure. Don't give them the idea that you are perfect and that you have never faced problems. Let them see your humanity so they don't have unrealistic expectations of you.

When they are old enough, encourage them to make wise decisions appropriate to their age. This may mean that sometimes they make the wrong choice, but as long as they have all the necessary information before they make their decision, they need to learn to take responsibility for the decisions they make. You can be there to help them rectify the problem afterwards and show them how to learn from their choices, ready for the next decision. Be your children's greatest encourager in their lives and be their greatest fan.

I remember when my daughter, Ayanda, was three and her nursery school had its sports day. She had no clue that it was a competition and I watched her coming last in a race. She was very relaxed. I called out loudly to her and then I joined her on the field. As we ran together I encouraged her that we could do it and we ended up in third place. I was the only parent in the field but it didn't matter. I ran to encourage my daughter.

I shocked the whole school, including my husband, but Ayanda and I had fun. At her school, I became known as the running mother and was invited onto the PTA (Parent Teacher Association – a board that oversaw the smooth running of the nursery school). I released my encouraging fragrance in the sports field to help Ayanda release hers.

A FRAGRANT MOTHER IS HOSPITABLE

In *Romans 12:10–13* it says, *'Be kindly affectionate to one another with brotherly love, in honor giving preference to one another; not lagging in diligence, fervent in spirit, serving the Lord; rejoicing in hope, patient in tribulation, continuing steadfastly in prayer; distributing to the needs of the saints, given to hospitality.'*

The word hospitality comes from the word 'hospital', which is a place of recovery, refreshment, repair, care, restoration, healing, and rest. A fragrant mother releases a hospitable fragrance, refreshing all those who visit her home.

Your children should be the first recipients of your hospitality before you host others. You have no business entertaining outsiders, going out of your way to make them comfortable, if you treat your children as unimportant. If your children are not allowed to use certain utensils, then your guests shouldn't be allowed to use them either.

One of the ways I minister and demonstrate hospitality to my family is by the meals I cook for them. They know that whatever we eat is going to be good, regardless of how simple or fancy it is. As a mother, it's rewarding for me when their plates are empty and their tummies are full. I feel blessed that they have enjoyed, not endured, the meal.

I teach my children to appreciate everything on their plate. I don't allow them to be selective with what they eat because I refuse to endorse spoilt behaviour. They know I wouldn't give them poison because I love them, apart from the fact that we would all die together, seeing that we all eat the same food! Once we've prayed over our food, it's sanctified.

One way to help develop a hospitable attitude in your children is to involve them in the preparation of meals. This is the best way for them to learn and it is an important part of their training. My daughter, Lebo, started helping with meal preparations before she was three. She would always ask 'What can I do, what can I do to help?' I didn't chase her out of the kitchen with warnings that it is a place that burns children. Instead I would give her small tasks like grating carrots or cucumber, even though I would end up with ninety-nine percent of the carrot on the floor! The point is that she was made to feel a part of the cooking team. Now she is older she can do a little bit more. We should not crush our children's spirits when they desire to help. So what if the cucumber tips over? You can always cut another one. So what if the kitchen is messy? We all had to start somewhere.

Involving your children in the preparation and hosting of guests is another way of training them in hospitality. When guests come and visit, teach your children to be welcoming, accommodating and kind. Teach them how to greet people. Even the Bible says to *'greet one another' (Romans 16:16)*. When you greet someone you celebrate their presence with you. Don't allow your children to let anyone feel unwelcome in your home by running to their bedroom without greeting the visitor, as this doesn't show respect.

A FRAGRANT MOTHER KEEPS A WATCHFUL EYE

One friend of mine was very kind and generous to the relatives who passed by her home, always desiring to help them. This made her a very busy woman and, as a result, she was often unaware of things that were happening in her home. One day her helper saw a cousin coming out of the toilet at the same time as her little boy. When she started asking questions she realised that the cousin had been touching her son's private parts. In her busyness, she hadn't realised that abuse was taking place right under her nose.

Be watchful and teach your children that they should tell you immediately if anything happens to them that shouldn't, or if someone touches them inappropriately, even if it's their father, uncle, cousin, brother, aunt, sister, other close relation or friend. That person may say to your child, 'I will kill you if you tell' or 'This is just a secret between you and me'. This language is designed to intimidate and silence them. Ban secrets from your house. No one should be whispering into your children's ears. If a person wants to say something to your children, let them say it out loud for everyone to hear.

I know another lady whose daughter was bringing her boyfriend home and sleeping with him in her room. Her mother was completely unsuspecting until the boy was seen by the security guards as he left the house. She was devastated when she discovered what had been going on.

You don't have to be a policewoman to your children. Commit your household to the Lord and ask the Holy Spirit to quicken to you things that are going on.

Never assume that your children are perfect and doing fine. Do spot checks. From time to time, go into their bedrooms and check how they are doing. Allow them their space and their independence, but not so much that their room becomes a no-go area for you. Respecting their privacy doesn't mean staying out of the picture altogether. One day you may walk in and find condoms, or your daughter may get pregnant right under your nose and you are completely unaware. You may just think she is putting on a lot of weight by eating really well. Wake up and smell the coffee. Be watchful and don't allow the enemy access into your home.

A FRAGRANT MOTHER DISCUSSES ISSUES TO DO WITH SEX AND SEXUALITY

Fragrant mothers tell their children the truth about their personal development, especially as they enter puberty. It is important that they are aware of what is happening to their body and are taught how to handle the biological changes so that they're not caught by surprise.

I would encourage mothers to educate daughters concerning their sexuality and fathers to educate sons. In the case of single mothers with sons, allow godly men in the church to educate and influence your sons, helping to shape and sharpen them into becoming the men God wants them to be.

If you avoid the subject of sex and entrust teachers or their peers at school to enlighten them, they are likely to receive completely inaccurate information and misinterpret what they hear and act accordingly. In some schools where children are given sex education, they can become curious and end up 'trying new things' with their friends. Parents of those children may have no idea what they are getting up to, thinking their precious children are 'innocent angels', when the reality is that they are actually gaining far more worldly experience than they can handle. That's why it's so important that you teach your children about godly courtship and sexual purity, so they can make informed decisions.

Along with the training you give them, trust the Lord to keep your children pure for their future spouse and to continue to be pure for the rest of their lives.

A FRAGRANT MOTHER IS REALISTIC

Help your children to be realistic about themselves. Don't flatter them into believing something about themselves that isn't true. Flattery can cause them to meet endless heartache, frustration, disappointment and pain along their way in pursuit of a dream which may be totally incompatible with their talents, gifts and abilities.

The Bible says that *'a flattering mouth works ruin' (Proverbs 26:28)*. When you flatter your children, you are lying to them. Use the Word of God as the basis for truth, not your own desires or dreams for your children. Don't try to make them a miniature version of yourself. Many parents try to live out their dreams, or sometimes their lives, through their children because they missed out on their own opportunities.

Be realistic with your children and encourage them to pursue the dreams that are in their hearts. Release them into the destiny that God has planned for them. Pray with them concerning their dreams, but don't tell everyone what your children tell you lest, like Joseph in the book of *Genesis*, their enemies pursue their dream and it costs your children more than it should. Faithfully conceal their dreams in your heart until the right time. You can follow the example of Mary in Jesus' life who *'kept all these things and pondered them in her heart' (Luke 2:19)*.

A FRAGRANT MOTHER KEEPS CONFIDENCE

Sometimes your children will talk to you about their struggles and about things that are very personal to them. It is vital that you do not betray their trust. Once trust is betrayed, you lose access into their lives. Don't gossip about your children to your friends, even church folk. Your children should be safe with you in your presence and in your absence.

If they are a challenge to you, don't transfer that challenge to your friends. Talk to God because you could be sharing your heart with someone who doesn't like your children anyway, and you may be reinforcing their preconceived ideas. God trusted you to carry your children in *your* womb, not that of your friend, and He gave *you* the grace to handle them, warts and all.

If you really need to talk about anything bothering you concerning your children, let it be to someone who is spiritually more mature than you and who is able to bring balance without criticising your children. People will come and go throughout your life, but your children will always be your children. They will change and work through their issues, but the person you talked to might hold on to wrong information because of what you once told them. When they leave you, they will take that information with them.

Proverbs 11:13 says, *'A talebearer reveals secrets, but he who is of a faithful spirit conceals a matter.'* Don't be a talebearer; faithfully conceal their matters. What a privilege we have to carry everything to God in prayer. Remember that every situation is subject to change. Pray about your children's behaviour. God can change and influence their hearts. After all, don't forget that you were once a challenge to your parents – unless you came straight from heaven to earth as a cherubim or seraphim – and I doubt that!

A FRAGRANT MOTHER DETERMINES THE SPIRITUAL CLIMATE OF HER HOME

Create a godly atmosphere in your home by setting the spiritual temperature and teach your children spiritual disciplines. Spiritual disciplines are things such as studying the Word of God, prayer, fasting, worship, giving, solitude and other godly disciplines such as fellowshipping with other believers, getting involved in the church and serving. These never change, regardless of the season of life you are in, and there is always a need to practice them.

Demonstrate spiritual disciplines in your home and encourage your children to embrace them. Your children need to learn to hear from God themselves, otherwise how will they know His plan and purpose for their lives? You don't have to be *their* Holy Spirit who hears for them all the time. They need to have their own encounters with the Lord and not depend solely on yours. They need to have their own faith and belief in God and their own personal relationship with Him.

Teach them how to have a quiet time – to set apart time for reading the Bible, prayer and discussion. When they are younger, read the Bible to them and discuss the stories with them. Get their input and feedback. Some of the most refreshing nuggets from our family devotion comes from Lebo, my youngest daughter. We never belittle her findings, we just bring proper perspective when necessary.

The growth and development of your children needs to take place in a safe environment where no unhealthy ideas are fed into their minds through what they are exposed to. Monitor and determine the music that gets played, the television channels that are watched, and the books and magazines that are read. When it comes to the Internet, monitor the websites that are being visited. Put security features in place so that they are not tempted to visit forbidden sites should you allow them to use the Internet in your absence. Not every website, innocent as it may seem, is good for your children. Some websites require your children to sign up for membership in order to access more information in the 'members only' area. Before they sign up to anything, check it out. What they are signing up to could just be a time-wasting gimmick which discourages or may even damage social skills.

Watching a lot of television is another thing which, if left unchecked, can affect your children's social skills or pollute their thinking. Although it's good to encourage wholesome entertainment, avoid using the television as a baby-sitting device to keep your children quiet or occupied. Determine how much television you will permit your children to watch and then observe and assess the programs they are watching.

I once watched some popular children's story cartoons and, before I knew it, I heard the characters swearing and using words which we don't allow in our home, despite having the appearance of being sweet and cool, so I banned that programme. Just because something is highly animated and contains sweet little creatures like rabbits, teddy bears or kittens, it does not necessarily mean that the language it contains is also sweet and cute and that the morals of the cartoon are sweet and cute.

Sometimes children have been known to scream at night because they experience nightmares after watching certain programmes or playing certain computer games. These may have looked innocent but in reality are dangerous as they advocate violence and destruction of property by blowing things up or crushing things. Slowly, in their subconscious mind, children will begin to accept violence as 'normal', if it is packaged as games, and this acceptance will gradually creep into real life. It's no wonder that one day they might poke someone with a pencil or even a knife, because they've been watching such things for years on the computer or television.

I have a friend whose son started having nightmares. He would scream and sweat at night, and some nights he would feel as though he was being choked. He wouldn't go to school the following day because he would be so tired from the nightmares. My friend called me as she was worried and asked me to pray. As we were praying I sensed that this was caused by something he had been watching. I quizzed her about it and, when she checked with her son, she realised that they had hired a certain video game in which the characters were quite weird. Her son had started to see some of them at night. So they went through all the material which on the surface seemed harmless but was actually damaging and destroying them. They have since put boundaries in place and now check everything that their children watch. Not every popular new game is good for your children.

It doesn't matter what your children's friends have or are watching; your children are your children and it's your responsibility to control what they watch. Bear in mind that because a film has the correct certification for the age of your child, it does not necessarily mean that it is healthy material.

Whenever we hire a movie, I watch it with my children so that I can take the opportunity to impart life lessons from it. If your child is a teenager, it's good to apply the same principles of assessing first and, if you have trained them well, they should also be able to evaluate certain things on their own.

A FRAGRANT MOTHER INVESTS IN HER CHILDREN'S FUTURE

I once had visitors whose children had obviously not been trained to appreciate what they were given.

They came at a time when things were difficult for us financially, but we still went out of our way to entertain them. I prepared a very good meal and when it was time to eat, the children just sat there, staring at one another and at their plates. I was perplexed. Then the mother explained that the problem was the mixed vegetables I had cooked. One child didn't like peas and carrots whilst the other didn't like corn. Neither wanted sauce on their rice – it had to be plain. They didn't want beef stew and the chicken had to be fried or grilled. So I had to prepare an alternative meal for them.

The next morning they told us that the children didn't eat brown bread, which was all we had, so we had to go and buy white bread. At the time, they were 4 and 8 years old. And they were clearly in charge. It was an unpleasant experience for us, but we learnt what not to do with our children.

Can you imagine those children as husbands or wives in the future? Selective about what they eat, expecting the world to revolve around them and their likes and dislikes, and ungrateful for what they've been given. How would they relate to the Lord? Would they only serve Him as long as they got what they wanted? How would they conduct themselves? We need to be wise mothers and make sure our children are properly prepared for their future.

Another way to invest in your children's future is by carefully choosing which school you send them to. If possible, send them to a Christian school. Remember that not everything labelled as a Christian school actually *is* Christian so investigate the school's policies and ethos before sending them there, and check their statement of faith to make sure that it agrees with what you teach at home. What is taught in a Christian school should be a continuation of what you believe and practice at home.

While a Christian school teaches your children academic disciplines, it also develops their life skills and character so that when they leave school and proceed to college, university or wherever they end up in their career, not only will they be effective and efficient in their practise, but they will also be morally upright and responsible citizens.

I know of numerous examples of well-educated people who were let down by their character. I am sure you do too. For example, I know of a gynaecologist who molested his patients when they were at their most vulnerable state. I know an accountant who used his education to get involved in fraudulent activities in the bank, relying on his knowledge and skill to keep him from getting caught, but he was arrested in the end. I also once had a neighbour who was a doctor with a drinking problem that threatened his career. It was well-known that come month-end he would have to be carried out of the pub, too drunk to walk. In all of these examples, education was not the issue, but character.

Christian education is important – it may not make our children perfect, but it empowers them for life. I would rather empower my children than have society choose for them what to believe. Invest wisely in your children's future.

A FRAGRANT MOTHER IS TOUGH AND TENDER

I remember a time when a couple visited us with their 3-year-old daughter. She was clearly in control of her parents and seriously lacked discipline. She would pull things out of the cupboards and throw them onto the floor. If anyone tried to correct her, she would throw herself on the ground and scream while her parents just stood back and watched. When her mother tried to get close to her to bring order, the little girl would smack her. I had to tell the mother that I did not tolerate such behaviour in my home. That little girl was demonstrating bad behaviour to all the other children and she was not a joy to be around. She had no respect for authority and was very defiant.

Proverbs 22:15 says, *'Foolishness is bound up in the heart of a child; the rod of correction will drive it far from him.'* If foolishness is bound up in the hearts of children, don't try to discuss matters to do with foolishness with your children. Use the prescribed rod to correct them. Don't be hesitant to discipline your children when they need it. The Bible also says, *'He who spares his rod hates his son, but he who loves him disciplines him promptly' (Proverbs 13:24).*

Work with your husband concerning the disciplining of your children, so that they don't play you off one against the other. They should hear one voice, not two. Although Christian families use the same Biblical principles realise that each family is still unique and there are no two families that run exactly the same way. Decide the rules and standards you want to operate in your home and ensure that your children understand them. If they disobey the standard they know, then you need to discipline them in love.

While you should discipline your children, you need to be careful not to be excessive or extreme in your application and enforcement of discipline. You could defeat the purpose of discipline and end up hurting, hardening or physically injuring them, or even abusing them. With excessive discipline they could feel confused, bitter or discouraged and you could end up losing them to the very enemy you are trying to snatch them from. Ungodly discipline will never achieve the desired results; it will always produce the opposite. Obey God's Word and you will receive godly results. Correction and encouragement should always go hand in hand. For a flower to bloom fully it needs both the sun and the rain.

IN CONCLUSION...

Proverbs 31:27–29 declares, *'She watches over the ways of her household, and does not eat the bread of idleness. Her children rise up and call her blessed; her husband also* (rises up and calls her blessed)*, and he praises her: "Many daughters have done well, but you excel them all."'*

My desire and prayer for you as a mother is that you may raise godly offspring; that your children will bring joy and honour to the Lord, to you and to their communities; that as you diffuse a godly aroma, a sweet fragrance, into their lives, they in turn will reflect the glory and nature of God in their lifetime.

Psalm 112 contains a lovely promise for your children: it says, *'the generation of the upright will be blessed'* and that their *'...descendants will be mighty on earth'* (*verse* 2). May your children be mighty on earth. May they do great things that will benefit humanity and display how great our God is. May your children be future great leaders wherever they go and may they never lack any good thing. Success is their portion because God has good plans for them. Your children will flourish and continue your great legacy.

If your children have gone astray and things don't look good, don't give up. Continue to love them and pray for them. Remember you are only a steward; their true owner loves them. *Zechariah 10:8* says, *'I will whistle for them and gather them, for I will redeem them; and they shall increase as they once increased.'* God will whistle for them and they will come back. His ways are always higher than yours. He knows where they are and where to find them and He knows which circumstances to use to bring them back. Just trust in Him *'and lean not on your own understanding' (Proverbs 3:5).*

Continue to release a godly fragrance and one day you will be together for eternity. May your children rise up and call you blessed.

FRAGRANCE POINTS

1. Motherhood is a gift from the Lord.

2. A mother releases a godly fragrance in her home when she follows God's instructions on how to raise her children.

3. A godly mother creates a godly environment for her children to grow in and influences their lives with her godly lifestyle.

'If you as parents cut corners, your children will too. If you lie, they will too. If you spend all your money on yourselves and tithe no portion of it, your children won't either. And if parents snicker at racial and gender jokes, another generation will pass on the poison adults still have not had the courage to snuff out.' Marian Wright Edelman

---

CHAPTER SIX

The fragrance of service

One Christmas, the Lord gave us an opportunity to visit my sister Lilian, who lives in Stockholm, Sweden. We sat in wonder in her very big house and reflected on the life she is now living as a diplomat. We thought back to the days of her 'small beginnings' as she served our family. Her journey has not been easy. Although many people along the way didn't see her potential, I'm grateful that God did. Here is her story...

When Prisca, my firstborn sister, was in secondary school, my parents were not able to raise enough money for Lilian, their second born, to go to school as well. It was difficult enough already trying to cope on my dad's meagre salary for a very big family, so it was decided that Lilian would stay home and help my parents raise the rest of the siblings. The decision to keep Lilian at home was not easy, but she accepted it. There are very few sisters who can do that. God had good plans for her and He was training her for the future.

Lilian's daily duties involved waking up around 4.30 in the morning to get to work by 6.30am. During those two hours she would go on her bicycle to buy vegetables to sell at a market stall. A friend often accompanied her and sometimes they would hitch-hike to various farms to buy maize. She would order produce from different places to sell during the day. In addition, she regularly cooked food for my mother to take to another market stall to sell.

If sales were slow, Lilian would leave her stall in the market and go into town to find other buyers. 5.00pm was home time, but not the end of her working day. Once she got home, she and mum would take the food to sell at yet another market until it closed. Then they would come home with my dad.

My mother made children's dresses during the week, and at weekends she would sell them at local farms.

And, of course, Lilian would help. My mother often sold the clothes on credit using a notebook to record the transactions. Then at the end of the month she would send Lilian to collect the money. This money would help to sustain the family and pay school fees. Lilian didn't stay at home and sulk, feeling sorry for herself because she wasn't at school, but maintained a good attitude. She had hope in her heart that one day things would change.

When my sister was older, she also worked in various places. Some of her jobs included being a domestic servant for Salvation Army missionaries, working in a hair dressing salon and also as a messenger in a boutique. In all her jobs she demonstrated the same commitment she had whilst working with my mum. The family continued to benefit from her financial assistance and all her employers were pleased with her fragrant service.

God continued to open doors for Lilian until one day she was able to return to her studies. It was a dream come true for her. With great determination she studied commercial subjects which incorporated secretarial skills. This led to her employment with Social Services. Word of all her hard work and commitment spread in governmental departments and as a result she was employed by the Department of Home Affairs.

One day whilst reading the newspaper Lilian noticed an advertisement for a private secretary in Foreign Affairs and decided to apply. To her surprise, she was offered the job and was posted as a diplomat to Algeria. From Algeria Lilian was posted to Egypt where another of her dreams came true. She had always wanted to visit Mount Sinai where Moses received the law, as well as go to Israel and walk where Jesus walked. Both her desires were granted. From Egypt Lilian was posted to Stockholm, Sweden. The lifestyle she now lives cannot be compared to where she has come from – a domestic worker to a diplomat.

When you serve faithfully the Lord grants you the desires of your heart. Don't despise *'the day of small things' (Zechariah 4:10)* because you don't know where God is taking you and what doors your fragrant service can open for you. *Galatians 6:9* says, *'And let us not grow weary while doing good, for in due season we shall reap if we do not lose heart.'*

Lilian did not lose heart although she was born unable to see with her left eye. Lilian didn't allow room for self-pity or see herself as disabled and she did not use this as an excuse not to serve others either. Instead she was fully persuaded that she could do all things through Christ who strengthened her *(Philippians 4:13)*. She also believed her mum's encouraging words that everything would turn out right and that one day she would be a great woman.

Ecclesiastes 9:11 says, *'I returned and saw under the sun that – the race is not to the swift, nor the battle to the strong, nor bread to the wise, nor riches to men of understanding, nor favor to men of skill; but time and chance happen to them all.'* Time and chance are given to us all. Regardless of your background, or how you start, as long as you serve with the right attitude and develop yourself, opportunities will come your way. The fragrance of your life will be released as you serve others selflessly.

Jesus said to His disciples in *Mark 9:35*, *"If anyone desires to be first, he shall be last of all and servant of all."'* He also went on to say in *Mark 10:43–45*, *'Yet it shall not be so among you; but whoever desires to become great among you shall be your servant. And whoever of you desires to be first shall be slave of all. For even the Son of Man did not come to be served, but to serve, and to give His life a ransom for many.'*

I believe that the key to Lilian's present success is her willingness to serve others. Though she appeared to be the least in the family, the Lord blessed her labour of love. Today, God has made her sit in high places. She is now working with leaders of nations serving on an international scale.

Wherever you are, look for an opportunity to serve, whether in your family, community, or church. Everyone has something to give that can benefit others. There are some things that can only be done by you so don't deprive people the blessing of your fragrant service. Know that in serving others, you are serving the Lord. Jesus said in *Matthew 25:40, 'And the King will answer and say to them, "Assuredly, I say to you, inasmuch as you did it to one of the least of these My brethren, you did it to Me."'* Your service will be a sweet fragrance that impacts the lives of the people around you.

It doesn't matter how big or small your service is, someone will always benefit. Even the Lord Jesus demonstrated this aspect in *John 13:1-17* as He washed His disciples feet in an act of love, humility and service. He said we should do likewise. As you serve others the Lord will take you places you never dreamt you would go.

As we enjoyed our Christmas lunch with my sister in her home we blessed the Lord for raising her up and sustaining her. God has blessed and prospered Lilian, despite her beginnings.

Woman! You too can make a difference. Betty Reese, American officer and pilot made a great statement: 'If you think you're too small to be effective, you've never been in bed with a mosquito.' That little insect can keep you up all night, and God help you if it carries malaria.

FRAGRANCE POINTS

1. Don't despise small beginnings.
2. Your heart attitude will determine what you accomplish in your life.
3. Don't grow weary whilst doing good, for in due season you will reap if you do not lose heart.

'We won't always know whose lives we touched and made better for our having cared, because actions can sometimes have unforeseen ramifications. What's important is that you do care and you act.'
Charlotte Lunsford

CHAPTER SEVEN

Fragrance your workplace

Some time ago I received a phone call from a woman I knew, who had just been appointed as the Chairperson to lead a group of companies. She wanted me to glorify God with her, as well as to pray for her, as she was entering a male-dominated environment and her job would involve leading directors of subsidiary companies. She was feeling threatened and intimidated, even though she was highly qualified to handle the job. Fear was trying to paralyse her so we prayed together and rebuked it.

God enabled her to confront her anxiety and feelings of inadequacy. She resolved to depend on His ability and favour. Today she is a high-flying businesswoman who owns a farm, supports her local church and community projects. She is also involved in politics.

I had the opportunity to catch up with her when she had just returned from a board meeting in China. She told me that over time she has gained the respect of the men and women she works with and hasn't allowed anyone to put her in a box. She has worked hard to accomplish her goals and God is rewarding her diligence. This gifted woman is releasing her unique fragrance in many areas of her life.

Decades ago, some jobs were no-go areas for women as they were seen as 'male-only' professions. It was uncommon for a woman to become a pilot, and if a lady successfully completed the training it would be announced in the newspaper, 'First Female Pilot!' Women were not trusted with this type of position. Even when it came to something like driving a bus, people would point to the bus announcing that a woman was driving, as if warning people not to get on board. Others might caution you that, although there is a doctor's surgery close by, the doctor is a woman! In all these cases, the women's qualifications would be exactly the same as those held by the men, the only difference was gender.

It was difficult for women to flourish within certain chosen careers. They would have to fight their way through criticism, discrimination, persecution and the like, in order to advance in their career. Once they were there, they had to fight to stay there. It was not easy.

Of late there has been a paradigm shift and many more opportunities are opening up for women to pursue careers in areas where they were previously discouraged. It is important that women move along with this shift because God desires to lift them up to release their unique God-given fragrance and to effect change in their workplace.

I am reminded of Deborah, the first female leader recorded in the Bible to judge the nation of Israel. She was a prophetess and the wife of Lapidoth. She would sit under a palm tree and judge the children of Israel.

A judge was necessary at that time because Israelites kept forsaking God and His laws to serve other gods. As a result, they would be captured by their enemies and end up in bondage. They would cry out to God for deliverance and in His mercy He would provide a leader to guide them, thus restoring peace in the land.

Not only was Deborah a wife and mother, she also functioned freely in her role as judge of Israel and we can learn a lot from how she conducted herself in her workplace *(Judges 4)*.

Deborah was required to work with the army of Israel, yet she wasn't intimidated, neither did she exert her authority with masculinity. She didn't confuse who she was with what she was called to do, because her focus was not on her gender but on her function. She was determined to fulfil the will of God for her life.

Like Deborah, it's important that you know what your role is at work, why you were employed and what you are meant to do. You are there to provide a service. You were hired with a certain set of skills that are relevant to your job and you should release the fragrance that God has put into you as you do your job well. Your abilities form part of your fragrance. Not everyone's abilities are the same so don't compare yourself with anyone; just do your best. This is what glorifies God. When others see you and how you conduct yourself, your fragrance is being diffused.

If you work in a male-dominated environment, it is important to realise that some men may find it challenging to work with you as a woman and to submit to your authority, because in their homes they are the heads. Some men have never been exposed to an environment where women are in positions of leadership. For some men you could be their first female leader so you could face a certain level of resistance, but don't let that move or destabilise you. Don't be over-conscious that you are a woman.

The Bible says in *Colossians 3:23, 'And whatever you do, do it heartily, as to the Lord and not to men.'* Don't undermine your skills. You can make a difference, whether it be cleaning or heading a corporation, being involved in the ministry, teaching, working in industry, in law, healthcare, dentistry, etc. Whatever you do, you are valuable and contribute to the success of the company you are working for. This is an opportunity to release your fragrance. We must remember that the Lord is the one who gives us opportunities and promotion as long as we are doing our best.

It was God who raised Deborah to become a judge in Israel and, because God raised her, no man could put her down. When God raises you to a certain position, there will always be some who celebrate your presence and some who don't. No one can put you down when God has lifted you up, so don't let anything faze you.

If ever you face confrontation or conflict, don't respond emotionally. Emotions can be a huge liability when they are out of control and in one outburst you can lose the respect that might have taken years to earn. If someone gets angry or deals harshly with you, don't react by being angry and harsh in return. *Proverbs 15:1* says, *'A soft answer turns away wrath, but a harsh word stirs up anger.'* Conflict can arise because you are working with people with different temperaments to your own.

My pastor says that all conflict comes as a result of misunderstanding. Learn the art of confrontation and apology. Follow the proper procedure for handling a grievance. Don't be a cry-baby or use tears as a weapon to avoid taking responsibility for your actions. Refrain from using your monthly cycle as an excuse to be moody and not to perform well at work. You are a daughter of the Most High God, so continue to release a godly fragrance at all times.

Never compromise your moral standards in order to gain favours at work or for fear of losing your job. *'A good name is to be chosen rather than great riches, loving favor rather than silver and gold' (Proverbs 22:1).* If you compromise, you will lose your respect and your freedom. I once listened to a preacher who said,

'Failure to stand for what is morally right is a prelude to being a victim of what is criminally wrong.' Walk in the fear of the Lord and not in the fear of man. When you stand up for the truth, the truth will stand up for you.

Releasing a godly fragrance at work includes being punctual. When you are punctual you honour your employer and you are being faithful to God because you are not being paid for hours you haven't worked. Don't take sick leave in order to sort out personal business. Don't spend hours surfing the Internet, writing emails or making personal phone calls at your employers expense. Let your conduct be consistent whether your boss is present or not, because the Lord is and He sees what you do during work time.

When it comes to how you present yourself at work, dress modestly. Do not tempt your male colleagues by the way you dress. Remember where you are and clothe yourself appropriately so dress with dignity. If you are at work, you are at work; if it's a casual day, it's a casual day; if you're at home, you're at home. You wouldn't want to be a source of offence to others just because you choose to dress carelessly. How you package yourself can affect how you are received.

When it comes to how you conduct yourself in meetings or at work in general, don't flirt or give mixed messages. Use your mouth to speak with wisdom and don't get involved in clamorous or foolish talk. Let whatever you say minister grace to those who hear you. Don't gossip about your boss or colleagues or interfere in other people's affairs. Leave matters that don't concern you alone.

Keep yourself up to date in your field. This may mean attending courses, training days or seminars. Build up a network of people with whom to associate. This will broaden your scope of influence and creativity base. Read relevant books to help you stay informed. It also helps to listen to the news and to stay updated with current world events. Deborah was up to date with the current events in the nation of Israel. She wasn't sitting under the palm tree, eating grapes and being pampered. She was actively involved in the welfare of her nation.

If you are politically inclined and desire to be involved in politics, or if you sense the Lord leading you that way to impact and bring change to your community, join a political party that represents the views and values that you hold. Don't get involved if your motivation is purely that you want to be popular.

You need to have a conviction that you can be an agent of change and to have a heart for the people in your constituency.

Understand your strengths and weaknesses because the political arena can be a tough place to be if you don't have the muscle for it. Politicians can be quite vicious. Not everyone involved is motivated to provide a better life for others. Some are there for personal gain. The woman I mentioned at the beginning of this chapter is of the conviction that she can make a difference by being involved practically in politics instead of criticising from a distance without contributing anything. If you are not actively involved in politics, vote for the political party that represents your values.

Should you decide to change or resign from your post at work, make sure that you follow proper procedures. Work to such a high standard so that when you leave your standard becomes the company's point of reference for the next person. They should miss your diligent hard work!

Never forget that work is God's idea and He is the One who gives you the ability to work to obtain wealth. Through your work, let God be glorified. Release a godly aroma in your workplace.

FRAGRANCE POINTS

1. Do your work with excellence as unto the Lord.

2. Develop yourself in your area of expertise.

3. You are not employed because of your gender but because of your skill.

'It's a great loss if a woman achieves success only because she has emulated a man. Her focus should not only be to succeed but to maintain her womanhood whilst influencing society.' (Anonymous)

CHAPTER EIGHT

Fragrance in a time of loss

It was St Valentine's Day. Everyone was excited. My day was going very well until mid-morning, when I received a devastating phone call. One of our very close friends, who had been with us two days before, was dead.

He was a bundle of joy – very vibrant and influencing many people for Christ. He never came to church alone. He would always bring someone. He was humorous, down to earth and very respectful. He had just helped us put curtains up in my daughters' bedroom, and when he travelled overseas he brought me organic peanut butter from his grandmother's fields, saying that I should eat organic food. He made me laugh, telling me to use it economically as it was homemade! I wondered how he got it through Customs in his suitcase. He was a very close friend, but suddenly he was gone. He was in a car crash and died on the spot. I was completely shocked – devastated, totally unprepared for the news. He was young, healthy and strong, only 25 years old, single, and had great potential.

We visited his parents, who were shattered by this loss. He was a pillar in the family and brought everyone together. On the night of his accident he had promised his dad that when he got home from work in the morning he would help him do some work on the computer. Of course, nobody had any idea what was going to happen and his death came as a shock to everyone. I saw the helplessness on their faces. They had been attacked and robbed by an enemy called Death.

We are reminded in *Ecclesiastes 3:2* that there is *'a time to be born, and a time to die'*. The moment we are born, our blank death certificate awaits inscription, because the way to the grave is for everyone *(Ecclesiastes 9:10)*. Our days are numbered. We don't see the number written, but the One who made us sees and death is no surprise to Him.

Psalm 103:14–16 says, *'For He knows our frame, He remembers that we are dust. As for man, his days are like grass; as a flower of the field, so he flourishes. For the wind passes over it and it is gone, and its place remembers it no more.'*

Our lives are fragile and our human bodies can so easily be destroyed. Just think – a piece of bread can choke a king; even the most cautious driver can die in an accident; aeroplanes have been known to crash and kill hundreds in one go; earthquakes have taken thousands; disease can destroy a body within hours, infections within minutes. You may be fully alive one morning, singing the verse of a song, going about your daily business, but when Death knocks at your door you stop singing immediately and you may not even make it to the chorus.

I remember once having a sudden urge to go and visit a young man we used to attend church with. He was sick in a hospice. When we arrived, Osie and I noticed his Mercedes Benz with its personalised number plate parked outside. For the time we had known him he had been very prosperous, but now he was a frail wisp of a man, lying in his room, too weak to do anything – let alone drive his fancy car. Reaching out his hands to Ayanda, my firstborn, he smiled at me and whispered bravely, 'Aunty, thanks, you've come'. Not many people were visiting at that hour. It was just his father and the three of us.

About 15 minutes after we had arrived, he began to stare blankly and was unusually quiet. We tried to encourage him in the Lord but then he began to gasp for breath. He was trying hard to open his mouth and say something but he just couldn't. Osie left the room with Ayanda and went to call the nurses while I began to intercede. At that moment I didn't realise that he was actually dying. I held his hand and his father was crying, 'Please don't go anywhere my son; don't leave us. Who will look after me? I love you. I'm here. It's the voice of your father, please my son, answer me, why are you quiet on me?'

The nurses rushed into the room and drew the curtains, but after a few minutes our friend was completely silent. He was gone. His father screamed and called his name until the undertakers came. We observed a few moments of silence and then prayed. A young man, who had suffered for months, hoping for recovery, was gone. We offered our condolences to his father, feeling so helpless because there was nothing we could do to help him.

It was painful to see such a young life passing away, leaving behind a wife and a son. He had flourished like a flower, but the wind of death blew and he was no more. He was the first person to die in my presence. The sight of the desperation of his father stayed with me for a very long time.

Death is an enemy. It knows no colour, creed or gender. It doesn't even care about age. Babies die, young people die, middle-aged people die, old people die, the rich die and the poor die. No one can escape, for it is not a matter of 'will it happen?' but rather 'when will it happen?' And when it happens it always shocks us because it's one of those areas that we're not equipped to deal with. Death rips people apart and robs them of important and valuable relationships.

A little while ago, I witnessed a lovely couple getting married. We were involved in the wedding arrangements and we shared their excitement about their new life together. Little did we know that the marriage was not going to last very long. The young woman suffered from breast cancer, which became very aggressive. While she was having chemotherapy she remained hopeful and cheerful. We would visit her in hospital and pray and sing with her. One day, the medical staff thought she was at death's door, but when we started to sing the hymn 'How Great Thou Art' we heard a faint voice singing with us. Everyone was shocked. That marked the beginning of three weeks of recovery. She began to walk, eat and even dress up. It was lovely to see her improvement and during that time we had some lovely chats, shared the Word of God and continued to pray together. As she made progress, her husband, a fine young man, became very hopeful. He literally stayed at the hospital. When he wasn't there he was busy making arrangements to turn their home into a user-friendly environment for her, in preparation for when she would be discharged.

Unfortunately, things took a sudden turn for the worst. One night she had a stroke and her condition became critical, she was deteriorating quickly. Her breathing had changed and she was unresponsive, even when we called her name. Her husband touched her feet and asked me to touch them as well – they were very cold.

The nurses were called in because her pulse began to weaken. Everyone looked helpless – even the doctors who came to check on her. Her husband held her close, assuring her that it was him – the love of her life. He kept asking, 'Have you forgotten what you promised me, that you won't leave me? I've already started making arrangements for when you come home. And remember we are going to travel for Christmas. Don't do it, don't go.' But the room went still.

I decided to cut into the steely silence by reading *Psalm 23* because I could see that she was beginning to leave. I held her hand and said to her, 'Don't be afraid, the Lord is with you; just as He promised, Jesus will never leave you. He will go with you and He will lead you to the Father.' Within two minutes, she was gone. I was still holding her hand. We looked at one another – the medical staff, her husband and me – we all knew it had happened. She had left us.

I saw the agony of this young lover who had been robbed by the enemy – it had attacked and taken his beloved wife. There were no words which could help. We joined hands and I led them in prayer and then we sobbed quietly. I was moved with such compassion and felt so helpless. The battle that we thought we were winning was suddenly lost.

Death is like an antagonistic army that comes to violate us, leaving us defenceless. No matter how prepared we think we are to deal with death, it still rocks and shakes us because we were originally never meant to die. God created Adam and Eve to live forever, but when they sinned, the enemy, Death, was released on the earth. Even today, all we can do is yield to it and surrender the life it has taken. You will surely mourn the loss of the person who dies, but all the mourning in the world can never bring them back.

Two of my sisters lost their husbands and they were each left with three children to raise without a husband and father. I saw the effect that death has on families; how it disrupts the day-to-day living and running of the home. The children were longing for their father, and their mother had to cope with her own loss as well as finding the strength to encourage and support them. From these experiences I realised that once you are born, you will surely die.

Death has robbed me of children I didn't even have the opportunity to see. I struggled to conceive for five years, and after much prayer and waiting upon the Lord I fell pregnant. You can imagine how I felt, after celebrating that I would finally be a mother, to lose a child through miscarriage. And it didn't happen once, but three times. I know other women have been through far worse situations, but for me this was too much to cope with. I was angry and disappointed because I suffered the physical pain of labour as though I would deliver a baby, yet I delivered nothing. I felt lonely and ashamed; a complete failure, as if it was my fault. I couldn't face people, especially pregnant women. I felt that it was so unfair that I had lost my baby yet they still had theirs. I wasn't equipped to deal with such things.

There have been many other losses in my life, including some of my husband's brothers, friends, cousins, relatives, and church mates, but the greatest loss in my life so far has been that of my mother, who went to be with the Lord on the 2nd of August 2007.

My mum, Bessie Chimkupete, was a very industrious woman who loved all her children passionately. Mum gave us life skills, and the most important thing she taught us was to love God and love one another. We would always hear her singing to the Lord at home, especially when we gathered for prayer.

Mum taught us to be hard-working and hospitable. She instilled in us the importance of moral uprightness and, even though she was a passionate disciplinarian, she had a great sense of humour. She strongly believed that a family ought to stick together and all eight of her children were commonly known as 'your mother's child'. She related well to all her children and had a unique relationship with each of us as individuals, always making us feel that we were her number one or 'best' child. She would always say, 'All my children are number one!'

Mum was our greatest support. She encouraged us in our careers and relationships. If she didn't like something, she never minced her words. We always knew where we stood yet she never put us down. Even when we were wrong, she never belittled us or talked badly about us to other people, and when she was angry she would express it there and then. She wouldn't spend days avoiding us or not talking to us, making us feel rejected or unwanted, and if she felt it necessary to smack us, she would. Even though we would make mistakes, we always knew our mother was there for us. It's one thing to have a mother, but it's quite another to have a mother who is there for you through thick and thin.

Mum would always come to help us if there were problems at school and she would settle sibling disputes in such a way that we remained reconciled, whether we liked it or not. Our household ran very smoothly and she would wake us up early in the morning and strip off the blankets saying, 'It's time to clean the house. Open the windows! Let the fresh air in!' Such was our training.

I watched how mum took her church very seriously. She would honour her leaders, ministers of the Gospel and missionaries and their families, by making sure they were well taken care of. When it came to guests in our home, they were always treated with love and care. She was very generous. We had to be careful that we didn't lose our meal to one of the guests if we were eating too slowly!

Mum would take in strangers and beggars and feed them, which didn't always go down well with some of my sisters, because she was using the provision they brought her to feed all these people. In order not to offend us, Mum would give these strangers tasks to do around the house. Sometimes she would even hide the strangers and beggars or tell them not to come on days she knew we would be there.

Mum also looked after mentally disturbed people, which at times was a challenge to us. I remember at her funeral how we were all deeply moved when a mentally disturbed man she had taken care of brought her a bunch of red roses. That day he acted soberly, and through his tears he said, 'This is for Gogo because she looked after me.'

After she died, we helped to finish off a project she had started, which was raising money for 'Helping Hands', a fund to feed the poor, aged and orphans. Mum achieved her goal. She was the highest fund-raiser, and my dad and sisters collected the award on her behalf. Even in her death, my mother's life spoke and she diffused a beautiful fragrance to those around her.

Mum was very strong and we never knew her to be sick, until the last three years of her life when she was diagnosed with liver cancer. The doctors originally thought it was a benign growth, but as time progressed she just wasted away. It was heartbreaking to see such a strong woman grow progressively weaker, to the point where she struggled to move properly.

She was a very courageous woman and I remember, when at one point she was frail and very sick, yet she told my father that she would not miss a conference that was taking place at her church. In fact, she told him that if it meant she would die there at the conference, he should take her! The doctors tried to stop her but she was resolute.

For the last week of her life she was in hospital, on oxygen, but still she fought bravely. She never wanted us to be depressed so she would smile, sing her favourite hymns and pray with us. She was hardly eating and we could just hear her calling on the name of the Lord.

One day she decided she wanted to be discharged and go home. She knew her time was up, and I will never forget that day for the rest of my life. Her final prayer was, *'Dear Lord, I am now very frail. I cannot help myself and I cannot help my children. I now commit my children into Your hands. Let them not walk in darkness. Let them stay in the light. Let Your Holy Spirit surround them like a durawall. Let nothing evil befall them. I pray for them to remain united, to study each other and get to know each other, to support each other, to forgive each other, to help each other. I pray, dear Lord, that none of them goes astray. And let nothing separate them. Bind them together with Your love. I have no one else who can keep them for me. I am an only child so I commend them and their children and their families to You. Amen.'*

When her time had come, she breathed her last and slipped quietly into that other room, the room which we cannot enter until it's our turn to go home to be with the Lord. My father cried like a baby for his wife of 58 years, his best friend. They had travelled a long journey, ending up with such an amazing family. He had hoped she would get better, but to no avail. Her death was very sad for all of us. We prayed and sang until the undertakers came to take her body away. We followed them until they told us we couldn't go any further. We cried, hoping this was all a big joke that would be reversed. Without our permission a new season had begun – a motherless one – and it was extremely difficult for us. This ruthless robber, Death, had attacked our family and took our mother.

I really had no clue what it meant to lose a mother. We had shared a close bond and she was the pillar of our family. God gave her to us as a precious gift to express His love for us, to nurture us, to teach us His ways and the practical things of life. Now this amazing woman was gone.

Looking back, I realise that the deaths of those close to me that had occurred were, to some extent, preparation for this, my greatest loss. Although I had sympathised with the families of those who had lost their loved ones, it took the death of my mum for me to really know and understand what they were going through. I also realise how ill-equipped I was to handle the death of someone so close to me.

The emotions that followed were shocking. At times I thought I was losing my mind. I needed lots of support, encouragement and help to deal with my pain and I thank God that so many people were there for me. Now it is my desire to use my experiences to help others.

It is not God's plan that we lose our fragrance, even in a time of loss. *2 Corinthians 2:15* says, *'For we are to God the fragrance of Christ among those who are being saved and among those who are perishing.'* Being the fragrance of Christ is not conditional to the circumstances we find ourselves in. Even during a time of loss, we can continue to release a godly fragrance to those around us. Your loss may not necessarily be that of your mother; it could be anyone or anything valuable to you. Although the impact of each loss is different, the emotional turmoil can often be very difficult to deal with.

God does not expect you to ignore your loss, or to deny it, but He wants you to mourn the loss responsibly – that is, to mourn with hope to move on. According to *Ecclesiastes 3:4* there is *'a time to weep, and a time to laugh; a time to mourn, and a time to dance'*. Continuous grief can become Satan's tool to paralyse you if you don't recognise it.

Mourning the loss of someone or something precious should not remove the fragrance in your life, and that is why my desire in writing this chapter is to help you mourn with hope.

EARLY DAYS

The early days of my mourning were the most difficult because everything was still fresh and raw. At first I experienced an emotional shutdown which was a defence mechanism to protect me from the pain. I remember being shocked by my emotions, then feeling as though I had been ambushed by them. I would start crying whenever I heard a song that reminded me of my mother. If I saw an elderly woman walking along I would wish it was her and start crying. Sometimes I just wanted to hear her voice. One day I even tried to phone her, and when I remembered she wasn't there I screamed.

I went through a whole range of emotions and couldn't understand why I cried so much. I felt so sad, as though I had been abandoned. At first I was in denial, later on I had to deal with anger and disappointment, and then deep pain and shame. I felt as though I had been defeated, since I had prayed for my mother's healing.

Sometimes I didn't want to get out of bed and didn't have the energy to eat. I was numb, and completely confused by all the mixed emotions I was feeling. I know I'm not the first person to feel this way, and neither will I be the last.

It is crucial that you don't allow your emotions to crystallise you and harden your heart. Some people end up wishing they were dead along with their loved one. This is a dangerous place to be. Although it may be hard to see and understand at the time, there is life beyond the loss. Be willing to release your loved one and accept that they have gone.

I realised that, because I loved my mum, I had to accept that it was better for her to be in heaven than to be on earth in severe pain. That's what really helped me begin to let her go. Keeping her here for my sake, sick and dying in a hospital, would have been selfish. I had to accept that she had gone to a better place.

TAKE YOUR PAIN TO JESUS

Isaiah 53:4 says, '*Surely He has borne our griefs and carried our sorrows; yet we esteemed Him stricken, smitten by God, and afflicted.'* Jesus was *'despised, a Man of sorrows, acquainted with grief' (Isaiah 53:3)* so

He knows how to deal with it and He knows how to handle it. On the cross He carried our griefs and our sorrow. Jesus died and He rose again.

1 Corinthians 15:55 declares, *'O Death, where is your sting? O Hades, where is your victory?'* Jesus can take away the pain of death, and He is our ultimate hope for meeting again with all our loved ones who were believers and have gone before us.

When you take your pain to Jesus, He does not heal you by bringing back those you have lost. He made provision for sorrow, which doesn't mean denying grief but being empowered to deal with it. For every individual it is a different process but Jesus gives the ability to carry on living. You have the right to cry and mourn your loved ones, and it is right that you do so, but desire to move on with your life.

Continuously bring your emotions before God, taking everything to Him in prayer and asking Him for help. Remember that you have a Helper – the Holy Spirit – who is your comforter. He will remain your strength whilst the ground around you feels as though it is sinking sand. The Bible says in *Psalm 29:11* that, *'The Lord will give strength to His people; the Lord will bless His people with peace,'* and in *Psalm 73:25–26*, *'Whom have I in heaven but You? And there is none upon earth that I desire besides You. My flesh and my heart fail; but God is the strength of my heart and my portion forever.'* Strength and peace come from the Lord, and when you ask Him for help, He will help you.

ACCEPT IT

I had to be realistic and accept the fact that I now had no mother. She was the first person I had contact with in my life and the one who introduced me to so many things I know now – to God, to a life of prayer, to life skills. She gave me the foundation on which others have built. When I lost her, I lost my first mentor. Her fragrance affected my life and the life of many others. Although she is gone, the things she taught me are still very much alive. My children and even those that I mentor now are benefiting from her investment into my life.

CONTINUE TO FUNCTION

I want to emphasise the point that the loss of a loved one should not cause your loved ones who are still alive to lose you too. Then it becomes a double loss, because they end up mourning the one who has died as well as the loss of their relationship with you. For the sake of your remaining earthly relationships, desire to be healed.

When I was in sorrow, people nursed and supported me – friends and pastors encouraged me and prayed for me. I had days of 'curtains', wanting to shut everything out and stay alone in my room, but they would come in and pray for me. I still needed to be a wife and mother, to go to work, to serve in the church – to do what needed to be done. Part of me was limping but my fragrance needed to continue to be dispersed.

After some months of being crippled by my sorrow I slowly began to get better. But I determined not to hide my pain and, at the same time, not to allow my pain to hide me. I knew I would dishonour my mother if I lost my fragrance after she had gone to be with the Lord. One day what got me out of bed was thinking that if she were to see me and the way I was going on, crying for her without even bathing, she would say, 'What type of mourning is this that makes you not have your bath? What type of grieving is this? Get out of bed!' So I got out and had a bath.

God is not finished with you yet. The fact that *you* are not in the grave means that your mission is not yet accomplished and you are still needed here on earth. There are times and places when you need to be vulnerable, where you need to expose your pain – where you can be the real you and talk about your loss. Know and use these safe places that God has provided you with – the people with whom you can be open and vulnerable.

If you are a mother of small children, try to avoid letting your children see your deep grief all the time. Children see you as a source of strength – a symbol of love, binding the whole family together like a cord which cannot be broken. But when that cord is loose, everything is loose. When a mother cries her children feel very helpless; they want to help her but there is nothing they can do to make her feel better. They feel upset because she's upset.

Take your children aside and let them know that although you're upset now, you will be fine. Allow them to hug and cuddle you, as this will help them to feel that they can do something for you, and it will actually help you feel better! Continue to be available to your children as their mother. Don't let them lose you. Remember that it's difficult for a husband to see his wife suffer, and he may not know how to help you deal with your grief.

One night that my grief was so overwhelming and all I could do was stand in my kitchen and scream for my mother. My children didn't know what to do and ended up crying with me. My husband was taken aback and didn't know how to handle me. Eventually he called a close friend who came over. She put the children to bed, then took me in her car and we went for a very long drive. I cried and cried until I slept.

God blesses us with emotions and we need to use them, but they should not replace God in our lives, for they can become a shrine. The loss of someone in your life should not rob your family of you – a happy, healthy mother who is watching out for her children. Purpose to be present for your husband, for your children and for your extended family.

My mother's familiar fragrance is gone. But since her fragrance has gone, it has strengthened mine because I've grown closer to the Lord, and all I want to do is to become more and more like my Saviour, Jesus, to please Him and do His will. I am also determined to leave a legacy for my own children to follow when I finally close my eyes in death. By God's grace I will influence the lives that come into contact with mine with a godly fragrance.

Here are some scripture references that are helpful to read during a time of loss:

- *Nehemiah 8:10*
- *Psalm 30:5*
- *Psalm 30:11*
- *Psalm 31:9*
- *Psalm 116:15*
- *Isaiah 61:1–3*
- *Jeremiah 17:14*
- *Habakkuk 3:17–18*
- *Matthew 5:4*

DEAR FRIEND...

You've been reading this book, may I now ask you a question? What preparations have you made for the day you will close your eyes in death? Perhaps you have prepared funeral policies, a will and great savings. How about your soul? Where will you go if you die today? Whether you like it or not, believe it or not, that day will come.

God loves you so much that He gave His only Son Jesus, that if you believe in Him you will not perish but have everlasting life. He is the only way to an eternal relationship with God. The choice of where to spend eternity is made here on earth while you are still alive.

I encourage you to give your life to Jesus. You cannot release a godly fragrance without God. You need to be reconciled back to Him who is the source of everything. Maybe there have been things in your life that have tried to choke that fragrance. Be encouraged, God is not finished with you. There is hope for you.

Perhaps you don't know how to pray and yet you would like to consider this matter. Here is a prayer to assist you.

Heavenly Father,

I thank You for loving me and sending Your Son to die for my sins. According to Your Word I confess with my mouth that Jesus is Lord and I believe in my heart that You raised him from the dead so that I may be saved. I invite You to be my Lord and personal Saviour. Forgive me of my sins. I receive the power to become Your child. Your Word says if I call upon Your name I will be saved. I call upon Your name and I know You have saved me now. Amen.

Signed: ....

Date: ....

Scripture References:
John 3:16; Romans 10:9-13; John 1:12

Welcome to the family of God. Should I not meet you here on earth, I will see you in eternity.

CONCLUSION

Go on! Release your fragrance

Woman! Gone are the days where the word 'woman' was merely a derogatory remark! No matter who you are, where you are, what has happened to you, your background, colour or creed, rise up and shine, for the ability of the Lord is within you. Go on – release your godly fragrance and diffuse the knowledge and love of Christ to the world around you.

It matters that you were born, for you are destined for great heights! The Lord your God, your Maker, has great plans to use you to empower those around you. The Lord is restoring your dignity, for He fashioned you for great works so that the world may see His ability in and through you.

Stop apologising for being a woman, for through you many families on the earth will be blessed. Go on and release that special, unique and valuable fragrance that refreshes everyone. Go on and fill the atmosphere with a fresh aroma of love, hope, peace and joy. Use all your talents and God-given abilities to bless the world and glorify God!

'Now thanks be to God who always leads us in triumph in Christ, and through us diffuses the fragrance of His knowledge in every place. For we are to God the fragrance of Christ among those who are being saved and among those who are perishing' (2 Corinthians 2:14-15).

Go on! The world is waiting for you. It's time to spread your godly fragrance everywhere!

'I don't know how we survived so many years thinking of women as a separate chapter. We are not a separate chapter. We are half the book.' Rosario Green

---

If you would like further information or you would like to share your testimony about how this book has helped you, please contact me on this address: fatima@godlyfragrance.com

Acknowledgements

To my Lord and Saviour Jesus, thank You for releasing the greatest fragrance of them all – Your life and Your unconditional love. Your fragrance is truly spreading across the nations of the world. I don't have enough words to express my gratitude to You. Without You I am nothing and I give You all the glory.

I would like to express my heartfelt appreciation to my husband, Osien. Thank you for being my best friend, for recognising the call of God on my life and for supporting me and allowing me the freedom to operate as the Spirit leads me, and simply for loving me just as I am. I love you.

Thank you to my daughters, Ayanda and Realeboga for inspiring me and bringing out the mother in me. Thank you for praying for me and for the fun, joy and laughter you bring into our lives.

To my dad. Thank you for your love, encouragement, continuous support and care. I treasure the friendship I have with you. I am still to see a father like you on earth.

To all my family members – Prisca, Lilian, Peter, Constance, Tracy, Sevy and Joyce – thank you for allowing me to use your stories and for your support and love. It's greatly appreciated and I think you are just great. I wouldn't wish for another family. To all our children and extended family, thank you.

To my mum-in-law, you are the best mother-in-law ever. Thank you for embracing me as your daughter and for believing in me.

Thank you to all my mentors and women in ministry who have helped me understand my role as a woman and embrace my femininity, using it to glorify God. To the women I have mentored locally and abroad, thank you. You have all assisted me in my walk with the Lord. Thank you to all the pastors who have discipled and taught me the Biblical principles that have made me who I am.

Special thanks to Emmanuel and Edith for being there for us constantly, through thick and thin. Thank you for believing in us and for allowing the love of God to flow through you to us. Thank you very much for your help with this project.

To all the people who have helped me with this project, you have been a great blessing, facilitating the birth of this dream.

To my dear Pastors, Gerri and Michelle Di Somma, thank you for equipping me further through Bible School and teaching me the life of faith and obedience to Christ. Thank you for also giving me the opportunities for the gifts of God in me to be expressed, both in the church and in women's ministry. Thank you for your love and care. I just think you are lovely Pastors!

To the Carmel family, my local church, thank you for your love and support. May the Lord our God truly bless you and reward all your labour of love towards me and my household. I love you all.